TRADING YOUR LIFE AWAY

Do You Control Money or
Does Money Control You?

RICH HOPKINS

WESTBOW°
PRESS
A DIVISION OF THOMAS NELSON
& ZONDERVAN

Scripture quotations marked (NLT) are taken from the Holy Bible, New Living Translation, copyright @1996. Used by permission of Tyndale Publishers, Inc., Wheaton, IL 60189. All rights reserved.

Scripture quotations marked (MSG) are taken from THE MESSAGE. Copyright @ 1993, 1994,1995. Used by permission of Nav Press Publishing Group.

WestBow Press books may be ordered through booksellers or by contacting:

WestBow Press
A Division of Thomas Nelson & Zondervan
1663 Liberty Drive
Bloomington, IN 47403
www.westbowpress.com
1 (866) 928-1240

Cover design by Joy Hopkins.

ISBN: 978-1-4908-7860-7 (sc)
ISBN: 978-1-4908-7859-1 (e)

Library of Congress Control Number: 2015906987

Print information available on the last page.

WestBow Press rev. date: 02/12/2018

Foreword

This revealing autobiography of **Rich Hopkins** gelled in a holistic approach to mend the mind and spirit, creating a simplistic strategy to break the chains of any addiction. *Trading Your Life Away: Do You Control Money or Does Money Control You?* is for anyone who desires to be released from an area of bondage and wants to experience freedom. Familiar with family destruction caused by gambling, I was encouraged by his story, the scientific studies he used to explain his story, and Biblically-based references that are to help live the life God intended.

Diana Pignato

Stewardship Leader
Gateway Church
Scottsdale, AZ

In **Trading Your Life Away: Do You Control Money or Does Money Control You?**, Rich Hopkins allows you to travel with him on his personal journey of revelation regarding the power of money to control. Without realizing it, Rich was trapped by the "power of mammon" and its influence and impact in all aspects of his life. It was only when he saw the clear light of realty that he was able to break away from the grip of money and possessions and finally find freedom through the power of Christ.

In the Bible, Jesus says something very powerful when He states no one can serve two masters. You will with hate the one and love the other or you will be devoted to one and despise the other. You cannot serve both God and Money." Each of us makes a choice as to whom we will serve: the God of the Universe or the god of money. For many years, Rich chose to serve the God of money until the one true God got his attention and changed his allegiance and his direction.

Rich's experience is a challenge to each of us to seriously consider whom we serve. Are we following after and serving the wrong God? Are we aware of where that is leading us? If you are ready and willing to change, you will find Rich's journey from financial bondage to liberating freedom a pathway to peace. I hope you will take full advantage of the wisdom you will find in the pages of **Trading Your Life Away: Do You Control Money or Does Money Control You?**

Dave Briggs

Stewardship Pastor
Central Christian Church, Phoenix, AZ

Contents

Preface

The book you are about to read was actually published in 2015 as my autobiography. I wrote it to a specific audience: to my family to explain why they had an "absent" dad and to Wall Street-type equity and bond traders addicted to a sort of gambling spirit. My vision was to take it to the traders working the capital markets in the "City" of London. It is now two years later. I have come to see my vision needed a magnifying glass viewed while consuming an energy drink. Though I went to London in September 2015 with the desire to market my book and minister to London's traders, I was not prepared to tell my story. The follow-through was not in me. I didn't have the burning call to do it because in my heart I was ashamed of my life. The last two years have humbled me to the point of truly understanding the supernatural experience described below that shook my world on July 6, 2012. It was the motivating push to write the book as first published.

In this revised edition of the book, I am leaving my story originally told as is. However, it is no longer the subject of the book. The book's title is in two parts. "Trading Your Life Away" is my story. "Do You Control Money or Does Money Control You?" is the question and message to the reader. The subject of the book is now "money addiction". My life story becomes the <u>example</u> of the love of money addiction and is, therefore, the latter portion of the book. I am deeply indebted to Dr. Darvin Smith of Boulder, CO and YWAM for the education on addiction. Most importantly, I ask my family to forgive me for trading my life away. Being deeply involved in the lives of my family is essential to an emotionally healthy family, and I was absent.

I must emphasize that the central focus of the book is a relationship with money, the love of money. In its extreme form, it is revealed as an addiction. Yet, it is hidden everywhere in our economy through marketing techniques that entice us to spend, spend, spend. Recent studies show that the bottom fifth of income earners in the United States spend 40% of their income on what economists call luxury goods and 60% on what they call necessities. Read "The Love of Money Defined" chapter below.

The book is written mainly to someone whose focus, whose life goals and values, revolve around "money" or the lack of it. Do you have a job so you can be productive, helpful, and relational or do you go to work with a narrow focus of accumulating money? Can you easily give away what you have or do you live in fear of lack? Do you gamble to try to satisfy the need?
Read on.

Rich Hopkins
February 2018

Do You Control Money? Or Does Money Control You?

Money Addiction

We begin with the supernatural experience that shook my world and now creates the framework for my study of the love of money addiction. It was a drizzly Friday morning, July 6, 2012. My wife, Mary Ann, my Youth With A Mission leader, Judy, and I walked from our Holborn Viaduct flat in the center of London to a huge roundabout called Bank. We stopped at a tourist information plaque describing the buildings around the Bank traffic circle. Looking across the busy intersection of several streets, we saw the Bank of England and the old London Stock Exchange. Facing the Bank of England, the British equivalent to America's Federal Reserve, I put my hand on the plaque standing waist-high. As I began reading about the Bank of England, I suddenly stood frozen. A brilliant white light encased me. As tears started streaming down my cheeks, I clearly heard:

"You are under the same spirit that controls the City of London, the spirit of mammon. It will begin to come off of you; as it does it will begin to come off the City of London."

The spirit of mammon is the Biblical term for the love of money. In its controlling form, it is an addiction. The second part of the book looks at how to identify the love of money. Let's spend the first part of the book taking an inventory of **you**. Hopefully, you will be honest with yourself. You will see if your personality is susceptible to addictive behavior and whether the addictive love of money (spirit of mammon) could be lurking inside you. We will then "live" an example of it's control through my life story as a bond trader.

Let's look at YOU. Please answer "yes" or "no" the following twenty questions from Gamblers Anonymous to roughly gauge if you are bent toward a gambling spirit.

1. ____ Did you ever lose time from work or school due to gambling?
2. ____ Has gambling ever made your home life unhappy?
3. ____ Did gambling ever affect your reputation?
4. ____ Have you ever felt remorse after gambling?
5. ____ Did you ever gamble to get money with which to pay debts or otherwise solve financial difficulties?
6. ____ Did gambling cause a decrease in your ambition or efficiency?
7. ____ After losing did you feel you must return as soon as possible and win back your losses?
8. ____ After a win did you have a strong urge to return and win some more?
9. ____ Did you often gamble until your last dollar was gone?
10. ____ Did you ever borrow to finance your gambling?
11. ____ Have you ever sold anything to finance finance gambling?
12. ____ Were you reluctant to use "gambling money" for normal expenditures?
13. ____ Did gambling make you careless of the welfare of yourself and your family?
14. ____ Did you ever gamble longer than you had planned?
15. ____ Have you ever gambled to escape worries or trouble?
16. ____ Have you ever committed, or considered committing an illegal act to finance gambling?
17. ____ Did gambling cause you to have difficulty sleeping?

18. ____ Do arguments, disappointments or frustrations create within you an urge to gamble?
19. ____ Did you ever have an urge to celebrate any good fortune by gambling?
20. ____ Have you ever considered self destruction as a result of your gambling?

TOTAL YES'S: _____

Compulsive gamblers answer "yes" to at least seven of these questions. Now answer True or False to the next questionnaire from "Looking Good Outside - Feeling Bad Inside" by Curtis LeVang, PhD..

1. ____ I have been told that I have poor eye contact, slump my shoulders, or blush easily.
2. ____ I am more perfectionist than I would like to be.
3. ____ I get defensive when others criticize me.
4. ____ It is relatively easy for me to criticize members of my family, people at work, God, or myself.
5. ____ I don't accept compliments well.
6. ____ When I'm lost I find it difficult to ask for directions or help.
7. ____ When I make mistakes I feel bad for hours, even days.
8. ____ I find it difficult to trust that others will meet my needs.
9. __ When things go wrong I have a hard time accepting blame.
10. ____ I cannot talk to my friends and family about my fears and disappointments.
11. ____ I feel down, hopeless, and overwhelmed a good deal of the time.
12. ____ I feel that I get angrier or angry more often than most people.
13. ____ I find it hard to rest or relax without feeling guilty.
14. ____ I was teased and called names when I was young.

15. ____ I rarely reveal my feelings.
16. ____ If someone does me a favor, I worry about trying to return it.
17. ____ I am sure I have addictive qualities in my personality.
18. ____ I have difficulty holding a job or maintaining a friendship for a long period of time.
19. ____ As a child I felt neglected or abused.
20. ____ I have a hard time believing that God can fully love and accept me.
21. ____ I never allow myself to get angry.
22. ____ My family of origin did not encourage or nurture my self worth.
23. ____ I have great difficulty getting close to people.
24. ____ I have secrets that would surprise and shock others.
25. ____ I feel embarrassed or humiliated by certain things from my past.
26. ____ Growing up I received little of or no support or praise for my accomplishments.
27. ____ I have trouble praying to God after I do something wrong.
28. ____ When with my family of origin, I rarely feel as if I'm treated as an adult.
29. ____ I feel things must be done my way.
30. ____ I take myself too seriously.

TOTAL TRUE'S: _____

Answering True to 15 or more statements indicates that "shame" could be a root cause of why you are drawn to gambling and why gambling is probably unprofitable and degrades your self worth in the process. A very low score probably means you are in denial.

Shame says to your soul (mind, will, and emotions) that "you are not good enough". Rooted in fear, it is the result of not meeting the expectation or approval of others, or by being looked down upon by others. It produces a false identity that lacks the ability to accept compliments. You fall into a conflict resulting in either passivity or you strive for recognition by setting up performance standards for yourself to meet. No matter how hard you push yourself, you don't succeed. Fear grips you. Eventually you accept it. In trading/ gambling, you keep putting on trades that lose money. You try to "get it back". You start blaming others or the marketplace. You fall into helplessness. You are driven to keep trying to overcome the obstacles preventing you from succeeding. You keep trading/ gambling unprofitably, but can't stop. You feel worthless. You see yourself as a failure; you are in shame. Your "bad" decisions have made you a "bad" person. The gambling addiction has carved a gaping hole in your soul that needs to be repaired with love and acceptance. You need to give away what you so desperately are trying to obtain. Get the focus off yourself. Give your "self" away!

Trying to "work" your way out of your shame can lead you to become a workaholic.To assess that possibility, please rate each of the 25 statements taken from "Work Addiction -Hidden Legacies of Adult Children" by Bryan E. Robinson. Evaluate each statement as never true (1 point), seldom true (2 points), often true (3 points), or always true (4 points). Total the points.

1. ___ I prefer to do most things myself rather than ask for help.
2. ___ I get very impatient when I have to wait for someone else or when something takes too long, such as slow-moving lines.
3. ___ I seem to be in a hurry and racing against the clock.
4. ___ I get irritated when I am interrupted while I am in the middle of something.
5. ___ I stay busy and keep many "irons in the fire".

6. ___ I find myself doing 2 or 3 things at one time, such as eating lunch and writing a memo.

7. ___ I overly commit myself by biting off more tan I can chew.

8. ___ I feel guilty when I am not working on something.

9. ___ It is important that I see the concrete results of what I do.

10. ___ I am more interested in the final result of my work than in the process.

11. ___ Things just seem to never move fast enough or get done fast enough for me.

12. ___ I lose my temper when things don't go my way or work out to suit me.

13. ___ I ask the same question over again without realizing that I have already been given the answer once.

14. ___ I spend a lot of time mentally planning & thinking about future events while tuning out the here and now.

15. ___ I find myself still working after I have called it quits.

16. ___ I get angry when people don't meet my standards of perfection.

17. ___ I get upset when I am in situations where I cannot be in control.

18. ___ I tend to put myself under pressure with self-imposed deadlines when I work.

19. ___ It is hard for me to relax when I am not working.

20. ___ I spend more time working than on socializing with friends, on hobbies, or on leisure activities.

21. ___ I dive into projects to get a head start before all the phases have been finalized.

22. ___ I get upset with myself for making even the smallest mistake.

23. ___ I put more thought, time, & energy into my work than I do into my relationships, with my spouse or lover, and family.

24. ____ I forget, ignore, or minimize important family celebrations such as birthdays, reunions, anniversaries, or holidays.
25. ____ I make important decisions before I have all the facts & and have a chance to think them through thoroughly.

TOTAL POINTS: _____

25-54 Not work addicted
55-69 Mildly work addicted
70-100 Highly work addicted

A workaholic has a strong tendency toward addiction, especially money, food, and relationships. It is a life-long process characterized by self-esteem issues that can result in either over or under inflated perceptions of themselves. They have an obsessively one-track mind always thinking about work - a work addiction.

Tying together these three personality tendencies - the need for a release from shame and a workaholic addiction to money externalized through gambling - and you have a motivation to be a trader. This book refers specifically to trading bonds, currencies, equities, or commodity/financial futures, but "trading/betting" blackjack, poker, horse racing, football pools and "fantasy" games, or just about any game of chance when money is the motivating factor can become a gambling addiction. Some traders succeed to become multi-millionaires. I describe the true story of such a Wall Street bond trader in chapter The Mammon Killer: A Heart Solution of the Trading Your Life Away portion of this book. He suffered difficult emotional trauma until he found his way out of addiction by "giving". Sadly, most traders fail because fear and greed take them out of the realm of objectivity into unresolvable "self" emotion.

Trading Your Life Away is my true story - in detail. You can see how I developed the three personality tendencies that took my life away. Though I can't tell you from personal experience, I suspect you will find those tendencies in most other addictions. As you read my story from childhood in the 1950's to the Summer 2017, you will see the building of an addictive personality. Ironically, I didn't see the controlling extent of my gambling addiction until I really personalized the statements/questions that you answered above. I scored 16 out of 20 gambling "yes's", 19 of 30 shame "true's", and 79 of 100 on work addiction. They are extreme scores for a shame-based workaholic addiction to "getting" money. Money has been truly controlling me.

For forty years money has had control over my life. What a sobering thought!!!! A supernatural "voice" told me that same thing while looking at the Bank of England in the City of London on July 6, 2012.

The supernatural presence of God came upon me again in the Summer of 2017, five years after London. I had just completed an expensive six-month ordeal replacing my teeth, leaving the bank account nearly empty. (We don't live on credit card funding.) In late June, a close friend, Kevin Zadai, gave me a copy of a his new book on the "supernatural". He has had far more supernatural occurrences than I. Even though I did not physically die and come back to life like Kevin, my encounter from death to life is just as radical. As I began reading his book, YOUR HIDDEN DESTINY REVEALED: The Heavenly Encounters Series: Volume 2, my wife and I were unexpectedly given airplane tickets to Kona, Hawaii and a place to stay just outside the University of the Nations (YWAM) campus for the month of July 2017.

What looked like a bleak summer in the 110 degree heat of the Arizona desert became Hawaiian rest and relaxation. It became our "meeting with God" that Kevin talks about in his book. God got my attention! We listened to mentoring sessions by Graham Cooke entitled "Developing Your Destiny". My life of hiding in the shadows came full circle. New relationships formed as I "gave" to others and began to listen to their heart cries. My quiet times were strengthened. New faith surfaced as I searched out truth. As I read Kevin's new book on the supernatural presence of God, I became aware of His Presence as my heart and mind opened to a change of attitude - a sort of freedom within me. With that, however, came an internal obligation to be obedient to my inner voice as well.

As I said above, publishing this book in 2015 was premature. We told too many people I was writing it. After three years it became embarrassing; I had to print something. Shame was lurking. I published it knowing I would have to rewrite it. Yet redemption was knocking at the door. While in Kona I met with a well-known writer at the University of the Nations Writer's School, for advice. She encouraged me to go forward, but with some helpful suggestions. I was similarly encouraged a few months earlier when I met at a Kansas City YWAM conference a noted psychiatrist specializing in addiction. I knew it was no coincidence and began studying the subject. I wanted to help a friend who had to leave his law practice because he innocently became addicted to a painkiller drug. Further confirmation came when I returned home to Phoenix from Kona. I was asked to support a friend leading an Alcoholics Anonymous-type addiction recovery group. This chain of events was supernaturally happening to show me that I, me, the author, had a destructive addiction to trading. When I saw my life for what it really was, I knew what to do. STOP TRADING. I did, but not without temptations. The key was to accept myself with all my flaws. I walked away from my shame. How? I focused on others to help them, not myself in comparison to them.

In a God-ordained encounter that confirmed why we were "sent" to the Big Island, Kona, Hawaii, one of the relationships I developed during that visit was with a man from Japan. He was overly preoccupied with trading - a gambling addiction. Common in the Japanese culture is "karoshi", an extreme workaholism. Such was his life. As I got to know him, I learned that he suffered from what I described in a later chapter on my "family life". We both grew up with an "absent Dad". Both his Dad and mine climbed the corporate ladder to "success" and left little focus for their son. My absent Dad, now deceased, left me looking for my identity in my work, sixty-five hours a week of "work" that became an addiction. My Japanese friend was going in the same direction - financial market gambling. Hearing my story offered him hope of a way out of his addiction. He led his Dad to a committed personal relationship with Jesus Christ. They were then connected spiritually and could receive the love of the Father in their relationship. Together their lives changed. Their relationship was now based on love and acceptance. There was no need for my friend to be driven to workaholism and/or a gambling addiction.

You, too, can walk away from the beginning of a gambling addiction. It is the spirit of mammon controlling you. If you will allow me to oversimplify this striving for money/recognition, it is a spiritual issue that should be addressed spiritually. You must recognize and accept who you <u>really</u> are, not who you are trying to be. Answer again the three sets of personality questions/statements earlier in the book. Before you get into a drug-centered treatment program, honestly examine what is missing in your life. Ask your relationships to help you. Be humble. Step away from your routines and rest your soul. No performance. No fear of failure. Don't be in a hurry to allow drugs to be the answer. Trust God to show you.

If you are a victim of hardcore gambling, the key to overcoming the love of money addiction is to recognize it's destructive power over you and then to take disciplined steps to overcome. Like most spiritual issues, its resolution occurs through human relationships. You must be able to express your emotions - to let it out - in a safe way and to receive feedback and support in an atmosphere of love and acceptance. To respond to this need, literally millions of hurting men and women have shared their lives in an Alcoholics Anonymous-type "twelve-step" program. Wikipedia describes it as "a set of guiding principles outlining a course of action for recovery from addiction, compulsion, or other behavioral problems. As summarized by the American Psychological Association, the process involves the following:

- admitting one cannot control one's alcoholism, addiction or compulsion;
- recognizing a higher power that can give strength;
- examining past errors with the help of a sponsor (experienced member);
- making amends for these errors;
- learning to live a new life with a new code of behavior;
- helping others who suffer from the same alcoholism, addictions or compulsions."

It is believed that the root cause of addiction is self-centeredness. You are self-consumed under the control of the addiction. Admit it openly. Shift your empathy from yourself to others. Getting the focus off you will soften the addiction control. Again, relationship with others is a key to loosening the grip of the love of money as well as the dozens of other addictive behaviors that Twelve Step programs have been formed to address. Just a few of them include compulsive hoarding, eating disorders, hyperactivity, insomnia, lack of motivation, procrastination, laziness, suicide attempts, depression, and fear. When assessing your addictive behavior, look for a controlling spirit inside you that makes you keep doing it.

Now that you have found what is "controlling" your life, you need someone to help you take control and get your life back. Trying to do it yourself may <u>add</u> addictive behavior and make it worse. Gambling is an addiction to (love of) money. Since you can't eliminate money from your life like you can alcohol, you need to learn how to develop a balanced healthy relationship to it. See The Love of Money Defined chapter below. Jesus talked about the love of money two thousand years ago. It was as strong then as it is now.

You need help to develop a proper relationship with money, which is the purpose of this book. You must understand, however, that just reading this book won't develop that proper relationship with the source of your addiction. A lifestyle change will be necessary to avoid places and situations that can trigger your urge to gamble. You need spiritual help & direction. Gambling is a spirit that must be overcome with spiritual authority. Most helpful is a support network of loyal listening relationships who personally care, fill you with that spiritual authority, and hold you accountable. Gamblers Anonymous's Twelve Step program would be a good place to start. You can also attend group or individual outpatient rehab classes at a medical facility. For more one-on-one treatment, try psychotherapy or cognitive behavior theory sessions to delve deeper into personality issues. Lastly, and least desirable by far, would be drug treatment to control impulses. Spend some time on the internet to find locations of help centers in your area. Read about gambling addiction <u>before</u> it becomes an addiction.

Now, as a quick "by-the-way", the State Street Center for Applied Research, a Boston-based research arm of one of the world's leading providers of financial services to institutional investors, conducted a study about the effect of the love of money on investor behavior. "Money-loving investors tend to think more short-term and are more prone to fear- and greed-based behaviors, which ultimately means buying high and selling low. In fact, when respondents were asked to choose between $1,000 now or $1,900 in five years, (assuming a low inflation environment), those with high love of money score more often chose the former. They are also more likely to believe that saving can be done later in life, typically delaying their contributions to a retirement plan, and putting away less than 6% when they do begin to save. Inversely, investors that exhibit less of an attachment to money make better investment decisions that lead to better financial outcomes, especially in the long-term." The author, Susan Duncan, concludes by saying that "emotional attachment to money exacerbates investors' behavioral biases leading to worse financial outcomes. The good news is that the love of money isn't permanent. The study found that while 67% of Generation Y respondents scored high in the love of money addiction, only 62% of the Generation X consumers surveyed were lovers of money. The percentage decreases further for Baby Boomers, who report 48%. As we age our priorities change and we learn that maybe money really doesn't buy happiness."

Are you a money-loving investor? Test yourself by answering the following five questions taken from the State Street study with the following point values: strongly agree (1), agree (2), neutral (3), disagree (4), and strongly disagree (5).

1) _____ I want to be rich.
2) _____ I am motivated to work hard for money.
3) _____ Money is important.
4) _____ Money is a symbol of my success.
5) _____ I like to think and talk about money.

Total _____ and divide by 5.
If your avg score is 1-2.5, you have a high love of money score.
If your avg score is 2.5-3.5, you are neutral toward money.
If your avg score is 3.5-5.0, you have a low love for money.

As you turn a page or two, you find the beginning of my 2015 edition of Trading Your Life Away: Do You Control Money or Does Money Control You?. It is the story of how I traded my life away. An addiction controlled me. I urge you to read between the lines and see how the symptoms of a shame-led desire developed into allowing "money" to control every aspect of my life and how I dealt with it for over forty-years. **Only now is it under control.**

Please contact me at rich@tradingyourlifeaway.com if I can be of help to you. God opened the door for me to teach lessons learned from some of my life's experiences through a Personal Finance course at a local college. I would love to share them to anyone who will listen.

Now on to Trading My Life Away.

ROMANS 8:5-11

The Message Bible

Those who think they can do it on their own end up obsessed with measuring their own moral muscle but never get around to exercising it in real life. Those who trust God's action in them find that God's Spirit is in them - living and breathing God! Obsession with self in these matters is a dead end; attention to God leads us out in the open, into a spacious, free life. Focusing on the self is the opposite of focusing on God. Anyone completely absorbed in self ignores God, ends up thinking more about self than God. That person ignores who God is and what He is doing. And God isn't pleased at being ignored.

But if God himself has taken up residence in your life, you can hardly be thinking more of yourself than of Him. Anyone, of course, who has not welcomed this invisible but clearly present God, the Spirit of Christ, won't know what I'm talking about. But for you who welcome Him, in whom He dwells - even though you still experience all the limitations of sin - you yourself experience life on God's terms. It stands to reason, doesn't it, that if the alive-and-present God who raised Jesus from the dead moves into your life, he'll do the same thing for you that He did for Jesus, bringing you alive to Himself? When God lives and breathes in you (as He does, as surely as He did in Jesus), you are delivered from that dead life. With His Spirit living in you, your body will be as alive as Christ's!

Trading Your Life Away

The Love of Money Defined

Trading Your Life Away is the story of how I lost the "life" of my life. I am somewhat embarrassed to focus on me because my life has certainly not been worthy of a biography. Quite to the contrary! I use the paper and ink to illustrate how a wrong perspective, a misplaced value, can take you down the wrong path and lead you into despair. My life story illustrates what it is to be owned by the love of money, both the fear-caused side of it and, to a lesser extent, the greed-caused side of it. The great news is that my story does not end there! Through a series of events, I've experienced tremendous freedom and liberty from its stranglehold. How I've wished that someone would have sat down with me years ago and shared with me the principles I'm about to outline to you. That's why this book is being written - to pass these keys on.

It was July 6, 2012, the "square mile", London, England. Three of us were standing at "bank junction" above the Bank Circle tube station in a drizzling rain looking at the Bank of England and the sixteenth-century Royal Exchange, the forerunner of the London Stock Exchange. I put my hand on a metal plaque describing the history of those icons of the financial world. Suddenly, my hand froze to the plaque, a brilliant white light surrounded me, and tears began running down my cheeks. I heard clearly in my spirit:

"You have been controlled by the same spirit that controls the City of London - the spirit of mammon. It will begin to come off of you, and, as it does, it will begin to come off the City of London."

Ten days later we had lunch with the pastor & his wife of a church near Hyde Park. I told them about the Bank Circle encounter. Tears started welling up in her eyes. She has been a main intercessory prayer leader in London's Christian community and in the political arena for three decades. She said that she has been praying against the spirit of mammon in London for many years. After meeting me and hearing what happened to me at Bank Circle, she said I was sent to London with an apostolic mantle to expose and oppose the spirit of mammon, more commonly know as the love of money, because of my experience with it and my twenty-year career trading bonds.

The Bible talks more about money than any other subject, so it must be important to the well-being of man and his relationships. Money, in an empirical sense, is simply a means of exchange - a dime or a dollar bill. But a reference to money can be possessively personalized to illustrate one's wealth or accumulation of assets. It can be a blessing or a curse depending on the spirit from which it is expressed and valued. Money can become part of our psyche. It becomes a spirit within us, creating its own outlook on life. That outlook controls our behavior and can even define who we are.

Do you control money or does money control you? Simply put, if money controls you, it is the spirit of mammon. Money controls a man or woman through the mind, will, and emotions - the soul of a person. Greed and fear feed the mind with abnormal thoughts that, if not recognized and disarmed, control a person's actions. The desire for more or the fear of lack are normal thoughts unless they compulsively run rampant and cause an emotional response. That response will usually be incorrect or inappropriate. When you find yourself trapped in this compulsive cycle, the spirit of mammon is in control of you.

The healthy way to relate to money is when YOU control money rather than money controlling you. When you control money, you see money as a means of exchange - paying for goods and services. The focus is objectively on what the money is doing rather than an emotion tied to your self worth. For example, you may think at the store that "I've got to have this!" and buy it. Then you get home and exclaim "I can't afford to buy this!" and feel guilty because you bought it. You may even take it back. But you don't hang on to the emotions involved in the transaction. You are in control. On the other hand, suppose you find the box of cereal you like on sale 50% off what you usually pay and you habitually buy the cheapest box in town anyway. You buy fifteen boxes because they are such a bargain. You get them home and store three boxes in every closet and in the garage. The spirit of mammon is in control. In the trading world, it is in control when you impulsively put on a trade striving to make money without objectively assessing the risk versus reward of a potential trade. When emotions control the decision, it is the spirit of mammon.

In the British culture, mammon is defined in the Cambridge Advanced Learner's Dictionary as the force which makes people try to become as rich as possible and the belief that this is the most important thing in life. The mammon spirit works through two emotions: greed and fear. If you have a lot of money, mammon expressed through greed causes you to obsessively grab for more. Conversely, if you have little or no money, this spirit is expressed through fear that leads to stinginess and sometimes even withdrawal - a fear of lack. As a result, in today's world of media-driven wants & wannabes, the mammon spirit causes a failure mentality. Yet, in reality, money is nothing more than a means of exchange - be it a dime or a thousand dollar bill. When we emotionalize money into a human power, it becomes a controlling spirit, the spirit of mammon.

My life's "mammon" addiction comes mainly from fear and a spirit of lack. I hold on to what I have out of fear that I can't replace it. The addiction to mammon also comes out of greed. Ironically, I "lived" my career in the same industry that is commonly known for its extravagant lifestyle of power-hungry, self-seeking greed - Wall Street and London's "square mile" financial district - "the City". The spirit of mammon expressed as greed is the same spirit that is expressed from fear and the spirit of lack, but it is in a different package. From either source, it is a motive - a controlling addiction - that distorts reality. Innate internal values of right & wrong become distorted. You can "trade your life away" through greed just as unconsciously, just as destructively, as you can through fear of lack. In either case, the spirit coerces you to believe that you can buy happiness. Later I relate the story of a Wall Street bond trader controlled by money through greed and power. It is a very different perspective than mine on the "buy side" of the bond market - but a destructive addiction, nonetheless.

We are going to begin looking at my story by making the assumption that money can have an addictive spirit attached to it. If you have a spiritual relationship with money, it is based on one of two opposite motivations and values. You are either driven by a love of money, which is rooted in our society, or you are led by your trust in God for the provision of money and how to use it. The former, the spirit connected with "the world", is the spirit of mammon. Jesus said it is impossible to be both driven by the love of money and be trusting in God for the provision of money. You must choose which set of values motivates you. Mammon wants to rule forcefully by taking the place of God. It makes promises to lure you into trusting it, sometimes using instant gratification. In the long run, however, mammon is a counterfeit. God, on the other hand, is a gentleman. He does not rule over you. He is there to respond if you ask Him. You must initiate. You must ask and then wait. You must trust in faith that He will answer. You are not the provider; He is the Provider.

Below is a list of needs that the spirit of mammon tells you it will fulfill. We all have a need for each of these traits to some extent. Sound the alarm, however, when there is an extreme need for one or two of them and they are not being met. The spirit of mammon will try to force its way into your life to fill the need. It comes at an emotional cost and it still doesn't meet the need in your heart. The spirit of mammon promises you:

- significance
- power
- freedom
- independence
- security
- identity

The first section of the book narrates my life story and how I was influenced by those promises. A lack of a healthy identity has been a huge issue in my personality all the way back to changing schools every year as a child - eleven schools in twelve years. The hurt of my divorce and the loss of jobs left me striving for significance. Because of my military school days, I have always had and met the strong need for freedom and independence. My job at Cal PERS was one of the most powerful in the buy side of the bond market, yet I never was conscious of using that power. I was more concerned with doing the best I could do (getting the best price), lest I would, in a strange sort of way, be defeated. My need for security and identity led me into a paranoiac fear that Wall Street was taking advantage of me. As you read my story, you can track how these six sources of the love of money (mammon) influenced my personality and led to an addiction.

Is the chase for money your god? If you have a feeling deep inside that you are enslaved, even addicted to an emotionally-controlling drive that wants "more and more", then you must read the story of my life. I tried for thirty-five years to reach the goal of that drive and never found it. Why? In reality, there is no goal. It is the spirit of mammon - a spirit from the pit of hell that deceives you, stealing your identity as a loving, caring human being. It leaves you searching for "peace and contentment" in money that can't be found. If you find "you" in my story, the final section of the book will give you the opportunity to be set free from this insidious spirit that controls your life.

"Your eyes are windows into your body. If you open
your eyes wide in wonder and belief, your body fills up
with light. If you live squinty-eyed in greed and distrust,
your body is a dank cellar. If you pull the blinds on
your windows, what a dark life you will have!"

Matthew 6:21-23
The Message
The Bible in Contemporary Language

Controlled by The
Spirit of Mammon

Across The Pond:
A Supernatural Experience

My wife and I left our life of routines at home at the beginning of June 2012 to embark on a two-month journey across Europe on a shoe-string budget. After nearly a week staying with friends outside of Paris, we spent the rest of the month of June staying in Youth With A Mission "bases" in France and Germany. We spent the first few days in July with our son-in-law's parents in Weinheim, Germany and then on to London, arriving July the Fourth. We had target dates for arrivals at each destination in France and Germany, but we travelled without a detailed itinerary - only a plane to catch from Frankfurt to London on July 4.

Traveling "free" set us free. My wife Mary Ann and I related to each other with a new sense of freedom; what caused conflict at home was absent. We experienced together with excitement the unknown on the other side of the mountain. Our relationship deepened to previously unknown depths as we each individually had time to evaluate "who we are" to the other. Old wounds were healed; our love for each other strengthened as we each felt better about ourself and our relationship. It was a wonderful time!

For me, my spiritual nature came alive during those days visiting YWAM bases across Europe. I had been a "born again" Christian for exactly thirty years. Yet battling the spirit of mammon (the love of money) had consumed me as I fought an addiction to financial futures trading. It had become so consuming that I lost my first love, God. Without Him, I had no other purpose than making money in trading, and I had no vision of how to get loose from it. The Bible says that without a vision you perish. I was lost in a rut. Now, with no access to the financial markets, I left that part of my life, estimated by Mary Ann to be 90% of me, at home. As we traversed across Europe I found freedom. We trusted God together in unity, which is one of the secrets of hearing from God and doing what He wants you to do. We were both in complete peace.

Being in the European YWAM environment brought back the "yieldedness" I had for God back in 1985 at YWAM in Kona, Hawaii, as will be described later. At that time, I left the trading environment of Denver for three months and found freedom to be who I really was, the Rich Hopkins that God made me to be. Now, in 2012, after "trading my life away" for over thirty years, I was myself again. I had the faith to open the emotional prison cell door and literally walk out. I began walking out of the spirit of mammon prison with new eyes - spiritual eyes that saw the "good" in people. Compassion arose from deep within me to minister to the hurting people. I now wanted to listen, to uncover needs, and to help. Jesus said that merciful people are blessed because they receive mercy as they give mercy. I gave mercy by relating to people instead of the four walls of my self-imposed mammon-created prison cell. I saw the "inside" of people: their hurts, their fears, their emotional and physical needs. They were touched that I offered to help them and they received me because they could see God's mercy in my heart. They saw my honest attempt to understand where they were coming from and to identify with them from a caring heart. By focusing on others, I was taking the focus off myself and my prison cell. I found that my personality changed as I helped them. When I conveyed kindness and was cheerful, people responded to me with kindness.

They were happy to see me; I felt accepted. As I focused back on them, the cycle began again. It was the end of an aloof, warped "trader" and the beginning of a life of compassion, of international compassion.

So my wife Mary Ann and I were in what could be called perfect peace as we embarked on what was to be a "supernatural" experience in London.

We celebrated America's Fourth of July from airports in Frankfurt and London, and began a monthlong British adventure. With no expectation of what we would do or even where we would sleep, we were greeted at London's Heathrow airport that afternoon by two thirty-year-old Youth With A Mission leaders of YWAM's "Megacities" ministry. As we rode the "tube" to the center of London (the City), our leaders explained that we would live for the month in their "flat" at a church in the center of London, and that our assignment was to prayer walk the "square mile" City and work with the churches there to create a common vision for evangelism.

Mary Ann & I were in our mid-sixties, very senior in a ministry of twenty-somethings who were willing and expected to sleep on gym floors. We were willing, but I'm not sure we were able. We were thrilled with our British home and our assignment. From minute one we knew in our spirit that this was to be a "God deal", a blessing orchestrated by God. We even had our own bedroom!

I was excited to have the responsibility of praying for the "Square Mile", the Wall Street of the United Kingdom and Europe. It seemed so long ago that I worked in the bond market with Wall Street, but those trading juices were still in me. Back in the 1980's I had dreamed of working for Goldman Sachs in London. It was one of those missed opportunities that I probably could have had. It didn't take me long to discover that the Goldman Sachs's office was a block from our flat. I watched the limos and cabs line up in front of their office late at night to pick up the traders and salespeople who worked New York hours. Were their positions profitable? Did the salesman catch the big trade? It seems so long ago that I laid to rest that rocky twenty-year career trading bonds and hedging interest rate risk. But have I?

The morning of our third day in London was rainy and unseasonably cold for early July. Mary Ann and I and Judy, our 30 year old YWAM leader, left our Holborn Viaduct Street church building flat for a half-mile walk to Cheapside Street and down to Bank Junction, the very heart of London's financial district, "the City". We soon walked up to a plaque on a sidewalk above the Bank Circle tube station. Resting on the waist high stand was a metal plaque that described what we were now seeing across the roundabout circle, the Bank of England and the sixteenth-century Royal Exchange, forerunner of the London Stock Exchange.

In a now drizzling rain, I put my right hand on the metal rim of that plaque and my hand suddenly froze to the frame. A brilliant white light then came over me and tears began to rain down my cheeks. I heard within my spirit a voice saying :

> "you have been controlled by the same spirit that
> controls the City of London - the spirit of mammon.
> It will begin to come off of you, and as it does, it will
> begin to come off the City of London".

What was the bright white light that makes it a supernatural experience? I don't know, but I do know it was real. I was surrounded by it for what seemed like thirty-to-sixty seconds. Something made me cry. My wife nudged me, saying "what's wrong?". I could barely talk, but quietly said "I'm under a white light". My hand froze to the plaque - I lost bodily control. In the scientific world, parapsychologists call what happened to me an 'exceptional human experience'. "An out of body experience is just being out of this body and into a body of light. Some researchers have even found a correlation between the intensity of the light experienced in a paranormal encounter and the extent of the psychological and physiological changes in the observer. We're talking about such things as curing of neuroses, lowering of blood pressure, breaking of addictions, and even the focusing of one's own healing energy." [1] I choose to believe in both my head and my heart that I did not have a paranormal encounter, but rather a visitation by God to set me free from the spirit of mammon. The Apostle Paul in the Bible (Book of Acts, Chapter 9) had a similar experience when God dramatically changed the direction of his life on the road to Damascus. I had a somewhat similar experience in 1982 when I became a Christian.

I knew that something critically important had just happened in my life. So, what was it that God was now showing me…was He now asking of me….that fateful, rainy July day in 2012…There I was frozen in time, at the very heart of that still proud city. What did it all mean? Was our month on the Continent "preparation" for our month in London? During the month we spent in London, I reminisced the dreams I had years before of trading for Goldman Sachs in London. Will I ever leave the bond market?

---

[1]   D.W. Hauck, "Alchemy of the Paranormal", Alchemylab.com, from a lecture given at the 1995 Whole Life Expo in Los Angeles.

Developing The Spirit Of Mammon: Traveling The Yellow-Brick Road

I was on vacation with my wife and three kids. It was 5:30 am on Thursday, August 3, 1991. I was sitting in a San Diego hotel lobby phone booth. News hit the wire that Iraq invaded Kuwait an hour before. Payroll employment should be reported bullish for the bond market the next day. I created mortgage backed securities from the mortgages my company originated. Wall Street wanted to get long the market because they too expected a weaker payroll report than they were officially forecasting, so they would give me a good price for our MBS securities.

For once, I had the inside track on Wall Street. My Dad spent a life with a major oil company, retiring in charge of world-wide exploration and production. Over the years, I heard him speak of the huge oil field they had in Kuwait. I knew Iraq invading Kuwait was a big deal, so I began selling mortgages to Wall Street in spite of the impending payroll employment report, which I forecasted to be weaker than the Wall Street economists were forecasting and thus create a rally in the value of the mortgages. Most of "the market" had no idea who Kuwait was or why it mattered. I did, and gave Wall Street what they wanted - mortgages - at what they thought were great prices. Guess what? Payroll employment was weaker than "expected" - and the market went down big-time when it should have gone up. I out-foxed Wall Street!

Such is the mentality of a bond market trader - always the contrarian trying to get the edge! I must warn you, however, that living the "contrary" life is not good for relationships; it is not good for your well-being. Say good-by to a normal life..... but I guess I never had a "normal" life!

Like many in America, my life story has been the quest for money. After all, that is an American dream. Be careful, as that quest can become a life-strangling death sentence that robs you of peace and contentment. When money becomes more than a means of exchange, it becomes mammon. The Bible talks more about money than any other subject. Why does it say that the "love" of money is the root of all evil? My story will answer that question.

I was born in 1947, which places me at the beginning of the Baby-Boom Generation". I used to say that if you find a need in my life, you will make millions of dollars meeting that need in my generation. I saw the needs, but never acted on them. I was distracted by the "spirit of mammon" and a blinding pride. And, yes, the "fall" came!

I grew up in a "corporate America" family. As my Dad climbed the corporate ladder, we packed up our keepsakes so the big moving van could come and take us to an unseen place, leaving friends and security behind. I went to eleven schools in twelve years. The only opportunity to have two-year school friendships was junior and senior years in high school. Unfortunately, it was not the typical high school; it was a rigid military school. Every minute of my life was controlled and punishment was severe if the rules were not followed to the letter. I was always goal oriented - to the point of being stubborn, which fits well in military school as long as the goal was the same as that of the school code of behavior.

My next step in life was planned several years in advance. I decided when I was eleven years old that I was going to Tulane University in New Orleans. My Dad was transferred to New Orleans from Shreveport, Louisiana. I sold soft drinks as a boy scout at a Tulane "Green Wave" football game in 1958. While walking through the campus to the stadium, I declared "this is where I am going to college!" In February 1965, I received my acceptance into Tulane. Life in military school then became beating the system that was unconsciously strangling me. I was on the golf team (State champs both years), so I had the excuse. I deceptively checked out of the military regimentation and checked in to the school's golf course.

Tulane was another name for the French Quarter. Technically, I lived in a dorm with a roommate. I reality, I lived in an apartment above Al Hirt's Place on Bourbon Street my freshman year. My sophomore year, a friend & I lived in a huge French Quarter penthouse with rooftop patio. We went to Tulane's freshman dorms and signed up twenty guys to pay twenty dollars/month to bring their dates to weekend parties. Our rent was paid and we met the ladies! My senior year was committed to dating/becoming engaged to my sweetheart as I lived in a Royal Street "slave quarter" apartment around the corner from the Morning Call. Chicory coffee & a beignet every morning! The only problem with that four-year picture - I was on scholastic probation until my senior year. Oh, but life was FUN, FUN, FUN.

One sobering obstacle stood in the way of a perfect life: VIET NAM. I completed the U S Army's "basic course" not once, but twice. I "slept" with my M-1 rifle in military school. Then I "met" it again in ROTC at Tulane. I was a shoe-in to be a 2nd Lieutenant in Viet Nam. I took the feared draft physical in the spring of my senior year, but I had a plan. I tried playing football in ninth grade. Somehow it caused my kidney to malfunction, resulting in a sharp rise in albumin. The doc back then said that I would probably never serve in the military. Remembering that, I spent the night before the Army physical walking the streets of the French Quarter to try to get my albumin up. I was also armed with a letter from that doctor. I wasn't even tested. The letter did the trick. I flunked the physical. I WAS CLASSIFIED 4-F.

I actually did graduate Tulane – and on time, June 1969.

A week after Tulane graduation I married my sweetheart during a weeklong beach party in Cocoa Beach, Florida. With a graduation certificate from Tulane in one hand and a marriage certificate in the other, I set out to conquer the world. Unfortunately, you don't conquer the world with certificates. Political science with a minor in philosophy was not marketable, especially with my grade point average. My Godfather didn't care and gave me a job in Houston. He was the founder of American General Insurance Company. He gave my Dad his first job out of college in 1939, and said "like father like son" in 1969, thirty years later. I was following the "yellow-brick road" seemingly without effort. The yellow bricks kept falling in place perfectly.

My godfather, Gus Wortham, asked me what interested me and I quickly responded "trading stocks". I spent much of my senior year at Tulane at the large Merrill, Lynch, Pierce, Fenner, & Smith downtown office watching the green electronic ticker tape on the wall for the price of "BE", Benguet Consolidated. I knew very little about the company, but I knew the price traded between four dollars and eight dollars a share. If I buy it at four and sell it at eight, I have doubled my money. I had little patience, so I would buy it at the low end of the range and sell it two dollars higher. After commission, there was very little profit left for me, but that was not the point. I loved to take the risk and win. However, playing the horses at the Fairgrounds was as good a bet, and I could drink Dixie beer while I waited.

Gus responded with a job in the Investment Department – a surprisingly small office of about eight people for such a huge insurance company. They actually were looking for someone to ramp up the department when I arrived. My political science degree and experience with "BE" didn't qualify me to be an investment manager. I began a study of establishing lock-boxes at regional banks for the collection of insurance premiums. I did spend time reading all the research coming in from Wall Street with great fascination.

The other certificate I received at Tulane graduation proved to be a devastating loss. Unfortunately, our marriage was nothing more than a certificate. My wife, Linda, and I were a dream team. Her economics degree landed her a good job in banking. Combined with my job, we pulled in great income. We began saving for a trip to Europe as our first anniversary gift to each other. That is, until Thanksgiving. Her mother came to see us. After three days, she took Linda home with her to California because she insisted Linda should spend all the money she made on herself. Separate account. Though commonplace now, this was 1969. At age 22 my yellow-brick road encountered a Viet Nam-type land mine. My naive mind encountered the spirit of mammon. The bridge over our troubled water collapsed. Our marriage became a toll bridge built on shifting sand, an insecure foundation.

I did not see Linda again for nearly ten years. The Texas legislature had just passed a law allowing divorce on the basis of "irreconcilable differences". My attorney, a fraternity brother of my Dad's, told me the new law was perfect for my circumstance and I consented. Unfortunately, there was no effort to reconcile – not even a phone call. According to her mother, it was her way or the highway. I chose what looked like the easy way – the highway.

When my Godfather saw what was happening, he got me into the University of Texas-Austin business school at the last minute - just before the spring semester started. Going to school this time had an academic purpose. Working in the Investment Department of a major insurance company opened my eyes to the education that I needed and I got it. Yet I still found time for my escape – golf. I got a job as a golf marshal at Austin Country Club. Harvey Penick, the University of Texas golf coach, was the club pro. Ben Crenshaw & Tom Kite were on the golf team. Great fun.

My other dream, going to Europe, would not be daunted. Through an international business student exchange program at UT, I got a summer job in Athens, Greece. My job four days a week was creating marketing materials for the Hellenic Industrial Development Bank. The other three days of the week I ferried to a different island. Yet hidden in the Europe dream trip was a tell-tale sign: I went alone, and I went for the specific purpose of experiencing and photographing the wedding church from "The Sound of Music" film that meant so much to Linda & me. It was as if I was saying "mother-in-law, you can't stop me from living my dreams". I sent the photos to Linda & her mother.

By going back to school I found the yellow-brick road again. The bricks fit perfectly again - for those two years. However, my arrival home from Greece was very difficult. I had no job lined up, no direction to go. I sank into the hurt of the divorce. I didn't have Linda to walk the next step with me. Life traveling the yellow-brick road alone caused me to stuff the hurt of a broken marriage deep into my soul. I emotionally went back to New Orleans hanging on to the memories. I got a job in the management training program at a New Orleans bank. To my surprise, my Tulane freshman year roommate was in the program. I barely knew him because I was in the French Quarter.

After two years in New Orleans, I moved back to Austin, believing I was healed of the past and ready to enjoy a dream job that got me back to investments. I happily agreed to work for an association of municipal bond dealers for two years with the promise that they would place me in the municipal bond industry in Texas at the end of my tenure. My job was to drive nearly every mile of highway in Texas collecting credit data on every political subdivision (cities, counties, school districts, etc.) in the state that had issued municipal bonds. I then published a report used by the credit rating agencies to determine their credit rating. I absolutely loved the job!

At the end of my term with a sophisticated knowledge of municipal bonds, I went to work for a Houston bank bond department selling munis to small "country" banks. The three years working in Houston set the stage to later destroy the yellow-brick road forever. I became bored selling muni's, seldom using the unique analytical ability I learned. The hurt of divorce came to the surface again as I relived our short marriage. I found myself falling into depression as I blamed myself for not fighting for my marriage. The "right" thing to do eventually catches up with you.

Then came the "8's of 86", a distraction I am living with over thirty years later. The U.S. Treasury issued a Treasury note debt security known as "the 8's of 86" with a guaranteed profit if you bought it at the "subscription" price. For the first time since I traded "BE" in college, I made a trading profit. The risk-taking trading juices came alive. I came out of the funk I had been in for several months. I asked for and received permission to trade the Treasury bond market for the bank. I spent every available moment studying technicals (price history) and fundamentals (economic) analysis. I spent nights at the Houston Public Library memorizing the Federal Reserve's Federal Open Market Meeting minutes. They explain the factors that cause the Fed to change short-term interest rates. I learned from data in the Wall Street Journal how to forecast the monthly economic statistics (payroll employment, retail sales, etc.). A Federal Reserve economist at the Houston Fed branch helped me learn how to predict the weekly money supply change using "demand deposits adjusted" released every Wednesday afternoon before the Thursday afternoon money supply release. Technically, I began keeping point figure charts on the Treasury 10-year note. After a few months I began writing a market letter sent to our bond-buying country banks analyzing & forecasting the economy & fixed income markets.

Trading is simply buying or selling a security, in this case, bonds (more technically, notes with a ten year maturity) issued by the U.S. Treasury. If I felt prices would go up for a period of time (a day to a week), I would go "long". If I predicted prices would go down for a period of time, I would go "short" by selling the security and borrowing the security from a Wall Street dealer so it can be delivered to the buyer. I felt prepared to trade intellectually and started going for it, performing well at the outset. I developed an analytical methodology and it worked. However, there is a human, psychological side of trading that I did not recognize. Fear and greed are the worst enemies of a trader. It is actually a false pride that says "I'm going to be right, just hang on." It caused me to allow a small loss to become a disastrous loss. Traders are taught to use a "stop-loss", a price at which I must get out of the position. I allowed my pride to say that I was right and consequently the market was wrong. I ignored using a stop loss that would get me out with a small loss because I feared the consequence of taking the loss. My internal value system became wrapped up in the greed of making money and the fear of loosing money. On balance, fear won. If I could do it all over again, I would require closer oversight – an even shorter leash – with stop-losses. They gave me just enough leash to hang myself. I was fired.

My response was to find the yellow-brick road. I bought an "around the world stand-by" ticket on Pan Am Airlines. My first stop was Seattle. After an interview for a job with a bank to trade 10-yr Treasuries, I ferried to the Olympic Peninsula for the weekend and a beautifully isolated beach hike. My next stop was to hike the Na Pali coast of Kauai, Hawaii. I called the Seattle bank from a lonely phone booth at the trailhead to see if I got the job. He said "YES. We will see you in six weeks. Have a good time." I found the yellow-brick road again!

Now in Seattle, I moved into a beautiful apartment on Queen Anne Hill with a great view of Lake Union, downtown, and Mt Rainier. I jogged to work at 5 am, but I was home at 3 in the afternoon. I loved Seattle. Unfortunately, trading at the bank was lackluster. I was, however, given the opportunity to do what I really loved. The bank's money market economist allowed me to write the weekly "market letter" to the bank's clients while he was on vacation. I correctly forecasted much weaker-than-expected GNP growth than the Wall Street economists had estimated. That hurt me politically in the bank and I lost my job.

So what happened to the yellow-brick road? It's gone - nowhere to be found. Gone forever. I spent a few months with a lady who had gotten close to my heart as we hiked the trails of the Cascades as - yes, at the same time - I traded bond futures for my own account. I found my identity, a bond trader with all its psychological baggage. All the beauty in the outdoor playgrounds could not match the thrill of pulling the "trade" trigger. Just as many traders resorted to alcohol or other fast-lane lifestyles, I tried coming out of my emotionless casket by walking amongst blueberries on the Cascade mountainsides. My lady must have really loved me to put up with my trading obsession - it controlled me. I became addicted to the emotional rushes, both up & down, of trading. I was totally obsessed with the markets, the strategy, and the trade. Unfortunately, there is not a correlation between the amount of emotional time consumed and the result. There is a compulsion to trade because you are so into it, which is exactly the wrong attitude. It doesn't matter how much you know. It is a roll of the dice. All you are doing is trying to increase the odds above 50% of winning. If you are wrong, get out of it quickly; don't wait around to try to prove yourself right. Also, don't "over-trade". Calculate the trade's risk-reward and take the most favorable trades. If I would have followed that rule, I would have been extremely successful. Instead, I wanted the emotional high, either win or lose. I put on too many trades just because I loved to "trade".

Yes, I made money, especially on my economic statistic forecasting. What a game Wall Street plays by forecasting the statistical releases so erroneously and, at the same time, positioning for the market move when their prediction is wrong, creating volatility in their favor. If I could forecast the stats so that I would be positioned correctly for the market reaction, surely the outrageously high-paid Wall Street economists could - and did. Unfortunately, I "overtraded". I put on trades that didn't have the winning odds. My "technical" analysis was supposed to save me from those trades, but it didn't. I made enough money to hike the Cascades with my lady, but I didn't get rich.

As the larch trees became their autumn bright yellow in the Cascades, I began to realize that I needed a job to further my career. Two months later I became the fixed income trader for one of the largest pension funds in the world, the State of California Public Employees Retirement System and, under an investment management contract, the State's Teachers Retirement System as well. The three years there became a PhD program in the bond market.

My job was to buy bonds. In the early 1980's environment of 15% interest rates, my assignment was to buy 8 ½ % to 9 ½% coupon corporate and MBS securities so as to insure call protection when interest rates declined back to more normal levels. I had some market-timing discretion, so I used my futures trading experience to be "in" or "out" of the market. I then used spread-to-Treasuries and corporate credit spread valuation analysis to determine which bonds to buy and at what price. Needless to say, we were an extremely large buyer in a market with few buyers. The Wall Street bond salesmen were constantly trying to get ahead of our strategy so they would have the bonds in inventory profitably or have them spotted in another client's portfolio when we came buying. What a game we played! My ability to wait and buy on weakness reduced their profitability, which I viewed as part of my job to benefit the employees and teachers of the State of California. I was always a buyer, so I focused on picking bottoms ready with a list of bonds to buy. <u>I was determined to be in control of an obvious adversarial relationship with Wall Street.</u>

My life away from the bond market did not exist. I lived two blocks from our office in downtown Sacramento, so I continued my Seattle routine of jogging to work at five in the morning. After eight hours talking on the phone to the best bond salesmen on Wall Street, I would unwind by jogging home for lunch at one o'clock. Then I jogged back to the office for reading/learning/projects. At 5pm, I jogged back home for a very simple self-cooked dinner and lights out by eight. My weekends were either spent at the office with nearly the same schedule or an occasional weekend escape with my lady from Seattle to Tahoe, or Yosemite, or the Monterey Peninsula, or the Wine Country/Sonoma Coast in California or up to Washington and the Olympic Peninsula, Cascades, or Vancouver, Canada area.

My life was extremely focused with no social life. After a year and a half of weekend escapes, I asked my lady to marry me. It was the greatest day of her life, she said. Six months later, she called it off and said our relationship was over. Even though we were engaged, I had never mentioned "wedding". I was too focused on job; the only time I could focus on her was our weekend escapes, two of them over the last six months of our relationship. She was tired of being taken somewhere nice in the hopes that a bigger spark in me would be kindled. I was passionless and insensitive about everything - except the bond market – even her. I could not share my life. I was full of a self-absorbing pride. I needed humility. I needed to think less about me and more about her. She ended my aloofness - our relationship was over.

What was the driving force that was possessing my soul? I was single, in my early-mid thirties, with no social life. That was abnormal in those days as my contemporaries all had families. My entire identity was in the bond market. I did not realize it at the time, but I was possessed by a controlling, driving spirit. I was still trading futures profitably for my own account with all the baggage that goes with it. Now I expanded it to include my job – a double whammy!

Over the three years at Cal PERS I became controlled by a spirit of lust known as the "spirit of mammon". Craig Hill, in his book <u>Wealth, Riches & Money</u>[2], explains that its purpose is "to get people to empower money with sacred value, thus making money their source of well-being in life." If you have a lot of money, greed causes you to obsessively grab for more. Conversely, if you have little or no money, fear leads you into stinginess & withdrawal. I was consumed with fear. In my job, I was paranoid that Wall Street would rip me (and Cal PERS) off. I was <u>driven</u> to buy the bonds at the best possible price. It required intense focus and stamina against an overpowering adversary - Wall Street. Unfortunately, I felt the same in my personal life. I became paranoid. I stopped trusting people in general and became isolated. I was condemned to the spirit of mammon.

---

[2]   Craig Hill and Earl Pitts, <u>Wealth Riches & Money</u> (Littleton, Colorado, Family Foundations Int,2003) p36.

Finding The Faith
Road: I Was Lost, Then I Was Found

By the grace of God, I woke up one morning in the Summer of 1982 with the proverbial "is that all there is?" moment. It was time to shake the dust off my boots & change my life! I asked my secretary where I could go in Sacramento to meet some single ladies. She encouraged me to go to a Monday night 600-member singles group at Capital Christian Center. I responded "Oh, no, no, a church? I haven't been to a church since I was in elementary school!" The next Monday night I found myself sitting in the back of a large auditorium (sanctuary) with tears running down my cheeks as I sang along with the soft melodic songs that I had never heard before. There was such a release of pent-up "something". I went back again & again and even started going to a Sunday morning service.

Within a month I received Jesus Christ as my Lord & Savior and became a born-again Christian. I promised to let God take charge of my life by reading the Bible and living by its teachings.

I had had some dates with a wonderful lady in San Francisco and thought what a great catch she would have been! However, God had other plans for me. I sensed that if I would trust Him, my_yellow-brick road would be replaced by a new unseen road called "faith".

We at Cal PERS had been managing both the State Employees and State Teachers Retirement portfolios. I was assigned the management responsibility for the smaller portfolios, one of which was the Teachers Tax Sheltered Annuity Fund. I loved it. When it became evident that the Teachers Retirement System was politically going to take their portfolio back in-house, I started looking for another job. My job was secure, but its content wasn't. I looked at a couple of jobs rather quickly. One was really of interest. I went to Houston to interview at my Godfather's insurance company, American General. Enter the spirit of mammon again, only now expressed as greed. We could not agree on benefits. Looking back, I was so incredibly stupid. Nearly every job I had after Cal PERS until I left the industry ended over my greed. In addition, during all those years since I left Cal PERS, I traded the futures market for my own account with little success. Paranoia increased. Yet, when I traded to give the profit to someone else, I always made money. Trading became an issue of the heart. It went from a spirit of the soul – mammon – to a spirit of the heart – giving.

During a period when I had no specific job prospect, I was referred by a Wall Street salesman to a possible job opening at a small investment management company in Denver, a place I had always wanted to live. I was ready for a "Rocky Mountain High". I interviewed the day after Memorial Day and a snowy 10-K run in the annual Boulder Boulder. During the interview I discovered everyone in the company was a Christian. I "knew" this job was from God and took it almost without question. My responsibility was to manage the investment portfolios of about fifteen Midwestern savings & loans. Take six zeros off the portfolio size I was used to running, but it was still what I loved to do. I drove by a church and heard in my spirit that I was to go there. The referring salesman had an investment property on a golf course that he gladly rented to me. All I had to do was start the car & get there. <u>I was on the "faith" road!.</u>

When I arrived I learned that the portfolio manager I was replacing took most of the accounts with him. I accepted the challenge. To keep the company going I had to find several new clients, so I started marketing where I had some contacts in Texas and Florida. After six months I had no new clients. My old nemesis, fear, began to grip me. Another ex-Cal PERS salesman helped start a firm in Denver and convinced me to be their strategist and "market-letter" writer. I left the job that God gave me out of fear that I would not succeed in finding new clients. Once again, I relied on my own strength and would not trust God. The spirit of mammon was at work in my life again. I ran off the "faith" road into a ditch.

A confrontation quickly proved that fear had wrongly driven me from the job I just left. I loved writing market-letters, so my focus quickly became designing a format for the letter. I thought the final product that I designed would be a great weekly letter to our clients analyzing and forecasting the fixed income and money markets, which I had done in prior jobs. It was my first priority and I developed what I thought was an impressively innovative product. When I presented it to my boss, the head of our subsidiary of a much larger company, he fired me on the spot, saying it was supposed to be a research report, not a "market letter". I was never given instructions of any kind other than what my friend who got me the job had told me. I aggressively stood up for myself to the President of the much larger parent company and he stood behind me, but I made an enemy out of my boss, who literally haunted me for the next twenty-five years.

Though I won a political skirmish, I planted the seed to loose the battle, the battle that became the war against my soul - trading financial futures for my own account. Not long after the market letter incident, I began noticing that between a minute and two minutes after every trade, the market would move significantly against me – every trade. It was no coincidence, I thought. I had no explanation until I discovered that my "boss" got copies of my trades as required by Federal regulations. I did not know at the time that his brother was the largest trader in the futures pit where I was trading. I lived in paranoia that His brother knew my account number. When the futures trading pit got the order from my account number, in my paranoia I thought he would signal huge bids or offers in the opposite direction of my position. The spirit of mammon sent me from greed to fear & back. I was paranoid, but I "knew" I could win. "He can't control me", I thought. However, by choosing to continue to trade, in my fear he did control me. The paranoia continued until the Summer of 2012.

As a result of that market letter misunderstanding, my position in the company was changed to bringing new clients into our upstart firm. I did my assignment and convinced a list of mortgage bankers, savings and loans, and residential home builders to sell their closed loans or MBS securities to us. They also followed my advice to hedge their loans-in-process through my market forecasts. I was using my bond market expertise and was actually quite happy until the parent company closed us down after two years. We were profitable, but the large bank that owned our parent wanted to sell them for its "servicing value" and our little operation was extraneous to that transaction.

Apart from my job – and now I was "apart from my job" - the missing element in my life was clearly relationships. My church helped nurture that area in my life. In the car driving to Denver from Sacramento for my God-given job, I asked God for the proverbial ideal family with "2.2" kids (the average family size) and a station wagon (which I already had) with Benji (the dog) in the back. A few months later I met a beautiful lady at church. Other than not loving dogs, she was perfect - a gift from God. Mary Ann is still the love of my life thirty years later. She had two attractive, well-disciplined, and most importantly, accepting kids, ages four and six. I loved them as my own almost immediately. God was in charge of that area of my life, at least. I was ready for a total life change – a complete makeover. It was clearly a match made in heaven!

We decided to get married after we each, separately, committed to a Christian short-term -missions organization called Youth With A Mission in Kona, Hawaii. For three winter months we allowed God to heal us of past hurts in a Crossroads Discipleship Training School. We both had plenty of hurts! Leaving Denver to spend three months in Kona, Hawaii was a case in point of the absence of fear. I trusted God. I easily got a renter for my home in the mountains. In addition, I wanted to rent my car, so I put an ad on the local grocery store bulletin board. The night before I left, a couple from Switzerland called me wanting my 4-wheel-drive car for the three months to ski Colorado. I gave them directions to my home and told them I would leave the keys under the front door mat with instructions on how to deposit the money in my account. I had no information on them other than their name and phone number. Well, the money went into the account exactly on time and the car was driven less than I would have driven it and without a scratch. NO FEAR.

But now the test. I had dreams of China right after I got to Kona. I seldom dream (that I remember), much less dream of China. The dreams stayed with me. Near the end of the second month, it was announced that our class would be the first YWAM group to go to Mainland China. I "knew" I was supposed to go, so I mailed a letter to my company back in cold, cold Denver asking them for six more weeks. They were not happy that I took off the time from work in the first place, but Congress had just passed a law that gave me the ability to take a 90-day leave-of-absence without pay and not be penalized for it. However, when I contacted them about an extension, they told me that I would lose my job if I was not back when scheduled. Well, I got so fearful that I returned early. Believe it not, the company was closed four months later. I missed the will of God because of fear. I made my job more important than God.

The good news: after two months back in Denver from Hawaii, WE GOT MARRIED.

We were a family of four living in the mountains, two of my dreams coming true...a real Rocky-Mountain high!

When the company I had been working for closed two months after we were married, I was full of faith. I went on many interviews to no avail, but I kept my chin up because I knew God was in charge; he wanted me with my family, not consumed in a job.. The job hunt went on for exactly a year. By then we were out of money. We committed to rent our mountain home and live cheaper in Denver. Two weeks before we were to move out, God gave me the perfect job doing the same thing I was doing in Denver, but in San Francisco with a large Wall Street firm. When I committed to leave my dream home in the mountains and trust God that He would provide something better, He responded. My wife & kids temporarily moved down to Denver and I got a cheap room in a downtown San Francisco boarding house. After a week in San Francisco, believe it or not, I met a couple going to Kona, Hawaii to the same school we attended, a YWAM Crossroads DTS. They let us rent their gorgeous Marin County house for less than our Denver mortgage payment. My family came two months later to a wonderful church and school – perfect for our family. My wife was three months pregnant – adding to our joyous excitement. Life was absolutely perfect.

We were on the edge of disaster in Denver, but we had faith in God to provide. He absolutely is a rewarder of those who diligently seek Him. We, as a family, were firmly attached to the "faith" road.

Aside from the working hours, the San Francisco job was great for a couple of years. Believe it or not (I keep saying "believe it or not" because unbelievable things kept happening to me), I shared my downtown San Francisco office with a man from our church. I even made money trading for my own account, probably because I was trading inside the large securities dealer I worked for. The drawback was the working hours. I got up at three in the morning to be at my desk by five, and I didn't get home until nearly six –exhausted. I spent four hours with the family and got five hours of sleep. Such was working Wall Street hours on the West Coast.

Life was great until the fear came back. The day our third child was born, I got a call at the office from a client. I called him from the hospital to learn that a mortgage position that he purchased through me was not authorized by his company and that the position had a huge loss. I was overwhelmed with fear. I thought he was hedging – that was his job. No! It was his personal speculative position using his employer's money. I feared that I would be blamed even though I did nothing wrong. My old paranoia came back; I was closed up and shut down. I had no faith; I was failing to trust God. Yet all I had to do was go on with the blessed life we were living. I had done nothing wrong. Fear quickly overcame logic. My trust in God began to disappear as the lawyers and depositions began to shake my tree. I lived in that crippling fear for a year. Eventually, I was exonerated, but the fear pulled the roots out from under the tree and I fled the scene.

A client in Phoenix asked me if I might be interested in managing their interest rate risk, but at a significantly lower income level than we enjoyed. As much as I loved the place we lived, our church and the kid's school, I emotionally had to change jobs. I was once again living in fear and paranoia at my work and I wasn't getting enough sleep. I aged twice what I should have. So we moved to Phoenix and learned to live on less income. Out of self-preservation, I said no to the spirit of mammon.

God miraculously showed up once again! He provided a wonderful house and church, and a great school for the kids. The transition seemed quite easy despite the climate & landscape change. It appeared that I had conquered the greed side of the spirit of mammon by accepting less money, but I left in fear. I was "leaving" more than I was "going to".

The first two years in Phoenix were very peaceful. The only negative was my futures trading. Without the "protection" of trading within a securities firm, I lost money on most trades. It seemed like Denver all over again. A rational man would not continue to trade…I thought… yet, surely, I must now have an addiction to it. I had to get rich quick, a motivation quite contrary to the teaching of the Bible. Clearly I was taking myself, and now my family, well off the faith trail by trading rather than trusting God for our provision.

In the fifth year of my Phoenix job, things changed. I was not paid the promised bonus. Ego and greed got to me as I insisted on getting paid instead of hearing their side and waiting. The spirit of mammon was once again an (the) issue. Even though it was couched in the preparation for selling the company for its servicing, I eventually lost my job as a result of the bonus issue.

While that bonus "thing" was happening to me, I got a call from another client from my Denver/San Francisco days, a friend in Albuquerque that I had been advising for eight years. He wanted me do for him what I was doing in Phoenix. When they offered a bonus formula paid quarterly, I accepted. But, unknowingly, I was being led by mammon. I had not first sought God. I sought money.

Unlike the previous two moves, I didn't wait for God to provide. I put it together. The element of faith was not involved. I was back off the faith road, and headed for another ditch. It soon became evident that it was not the will and blessing of God. We could not find the right house and had to settle for a small townhouse. We found little peace at the three churches we attended. Each church has its own personality & purpose. God sends believers to a particular church because they need the personality & purpose that it provides. In Albuquerque we were not "sent" to a church; we just "went" to different churches while we were there. I was routinely under spiritual attack. The only good thing I could say about our time in our "land of entrapment" was a favorable experience in high school for the two older kids.

In Albuquerque, life's events were negative like never before. I became afflicted with a palsy in my left eye that left me with double vision as we initially drove into New Mexico. That didn't just happen. It was a warning of the spiritual battle to come. The New Living Translation of Matthew 6:21-23 says "The eye is the lamp of the body. So if your eye is sound, your entire body will be full of light. But if your eye is unsound, your whole body will be full of darkness. If then the very light in you is darkened, how dense is that darkness!" The next couple of verses proclaim you cannot serve both God and deceitful riches, money, possessions, or whatever is trusted in. That is to say, mammon. My double vision was physical evidence of the spirit of mammon that resided in my heart.

There is more. The second week on the job I jumped off a fence and broke both heals, leaving me bed-ridden for eight weeks. Then, my daughter totaled our Volvo a month after the family arrived from Phoenix. Finally, the most tell-tale sign that I missed God's job for me: I learned a year later that my exceptionally capable assistant in Phoenix had changed jobs as the company for whom we had both worked was sold. She went to a small bank in Phoenix that wanted to start and quickly grow an operation like we had. She told them they had to hire me. I went to interview for the job, but I never was called back. A few days after the interview, the FDIC audited them and eventually shut them down because they bought a wildly speculative security that I never would have bought. Had I waited for God and stayed in Phoenix, I think that would have been my job.

It was no surprise that the Albuquerque job ended as uncomfortably as it started. The person I was hired to replace came back to work after a painful divorce. I taught him what I knew and then I was replaced. I came back from a college reunion in New Orleans to find that I was let go as part of a ten percent staff reduction. The man I originally replaced was my "trained" assistant and then my replacement. My bonus formula caused me to be way overpaid relative to the other employees. Mammon, mammon, mammon.

"Keep away from anything that might
take God's place in your heart."

1 John 5:21
Holy Bible
New Living Translation

Mammonized Family Redeemed

The spirit of mammon is a pervasive – yet silent – controller. Under its control I lived in a prison cell that I subconsciously locked. I isolated myself from my family through the excuse that I was making money FOR THEM. The reality, however, was that the mammonized family environment that I created was the environment in which I grew up. I had an "absent" Dad whose focus was climbing the corporate ladder. My focus was trading, and it absorbed me totally, just as the corporation did my Dad.

Mammon's control over me could be considered a family "curse" passed down from generation to generation. I remember my Dad keeping statistics on horses & jockeys so he could bet the races at the New Orleans Fairgrounds. I also remember him keeping college football stats to bet the weekly football pools. I think I even participated. He wanted to rent rather than buy a house so that he could use the down payment money to trade stocks. I wonder where the desire to trade/gamble came from. But, most telling, my Dad refused to receive Jesus because he would not give any of his money to a church and he believed that was required to be saved.

Another family curse is fear. I was recently made aware of it when fire damaged my Mom's forty-year-old house. The insurance company intimidated my Mom and sister with their initial settlement to restore the house. My Mom responded with a family curse. She responded in paralyzing fear that the cost of the renovation would go over budget, denying us improvements that are normally made to bring it to today's standards. As an interior designer, my wife has done several fire restorations. She tried to encourage my Mom that upgrades are part of the process, but my Mom remained in fear, both of the insurance company and of the mammon consequences of cost overruns. I have been similarly intimidated in the bond market many, many times with the same paralyzing result. Fear is the downfall of a trader. Why was I a bond trader?

New research in the field of neuroscience has developed the study of epigenetics - the study of how the mind changes the brain through the choices we make. It says that my life's outcome does not have to be the result of my family. Parents can create a predisposition, but not a destiny, for their children to live out the negatives of the parent's lives. If the son or daughter, no matter the age, assumes those negative thoughts and they become desires, he or she must take responsibility for the choice made and choose to accept, reject, or change that predisposition before it is relived as a destiny. Unfortunately, I was unaware of the need to reject/change when it was important to change and it became my destiny. Becoming a gambling bond trader was a natural, but it was my choice.

My distant relationship with my son could also be considered a family curse. My Mom recalls stories of how my Dad's dad could not relate to him, and, indeed, sent him to the same military high school that I attended. My Dad never learned how to relate to me because he never experienced his dad relating to him. I have carried the same inadequacy to my son. Fortunately, however, God's grace has convicted me over the last few years to stop the generational curse by sincerely apologizing to my son, making him sensitively aware of it. His relationship with his two sons is, and will continue to be, a strongly knit, communicative sharing of their lives. I am so grateful for the tender relationships he is developing - for my grandsons' sake.

I praise God for my family and for helping them overcome what could have been overwhelming emotional circumstances. Their biological dad went to prison for income tax evasion (spirit of mammon?) when the kids were two and four. I met them when they were four and six. I truly fell in love with them, which was quite surprising since I had never had relationships with children – ever – in my thirty-six years. We became a family a year and a half later, the same month their biological dad, hopeless & penniless, got out of prison. The kid's reunion with their dad seemed emotionless - as if their "absent" dad did not exist. Throughout the years since, I felt guilty, fearing I had "stolen" their dad. I encouraged them to see him. They had little interest, however, until they were teenagers. He passed away between their college graduations and their marriages.

The circumstances of our first year as a family were nearly perfect. As I mentioned in the previous chapter, my employer closed its doors right after we got married. My "job" became finding another job, which I shared with my new family. We lived in the mountains above Denver enjoying together the beauty of the Rockies with hikes, campfires, and berry-picking in the summer and sledding out our backdoor in the winter. We, of course, had "issues", but God supernaturally put us together. We were a family made in Heaven!

God's plan for us did not end in Denver. Our year in the Colorado Mountains without a job gave us time to knit as a family. When God thought we were ready to face the pressures of family life in America, He moved us to San Francisco. Because I worked both New York & West Coast hours, I woke up at three in the morning to be at work at my downtown San Francisco phone and trading screen for the 5:30 am economic releases that move the financial markets. I completed the workday by either driving or taking the bus to our

Marin County home, arriving home exhausted between about 6 pm.. I spent three hours with the family, an hour with my wife, and squeezed in five and a half hours of sleep.

Having had no experience with kids, I raised them as I was raised, including being the "absent dad". In my spirit I knew I was being an absent dad, especially compared to our family life in Denver. I tried feverishly to keep our close family relationships. I took my beautiful and poised daughter on "date nights" for dinner. I cheered my son at his soccer & whiffle-ball games. As a family we went to Stinson Beach or hiked the beauty of Marin County. But that was weekends. The three hours a night I had allocated for family time during the week was shared with our church and Bible College, leaving, in reality, just an hour a day for the family. I was the dad my dad was – except my dad didn't go to my sports events. My wife held the family together just as my Mom did for my family when I was growing up thirty years earlier. My wife's trust in God was the guiding light. She was a true "Proverbs 31" woman. I thank God for her – even more so today.

We lived in Marin County, one of the wealthiest counties in America at that time (the mid-80's). The spirit of mammon was the controlling spirit of the area, but God provided us the church to separate us from that spirit. Our social life revolved around the church. Our kids went to the church's school, so their friends were part of the church. God's provision of a house was meant to plant us so we would not succumb to the spirit of mammon as a family. As an example, our son's first grade teacher lived five houses down the street! Another example, we had another neighbor from our church whose dad had commuted to work with my Dad during the early years of their careers in the 1950's and both retired from that company about the same time over forty years later!

My San Francisco years filled the pocketbook, especially in personal trading. Because my trading was through an account with my employer, I didn't have the "opposition" I had in Denver. As my trading results improved, the paranoia disappeared. But please beware, however, the mammon spirit doesn't let go without a fight. The fear side of mammon shifted from personal trading to my job and my financial security. I relented to the fear described in the previous chapter and accepted a job in Phoenix. My family was so happy, as was I, in Marin County. We were in the center of God's will. How could I leave???? I allowed my job to be more important than God and my family. I was controlled by fear and disobeyed God.

To prove God's forgiving character to us, the move to Phoenix had the same kind of miraculous provision we experienced when moving to San Francisco from Denver. I moved ahead of the family by six weeks, just as before. God provided us the perfect house close to the perfect church and the perfect Christian school, just as in San Francisco. Even though it was hard for all of us to leave Marin County, once settled into what God gave us in Phoenix, we were very content and appreciative of the next step of our journey together.

As was the case in San Francisco, the years in Phoenix as a family revolved around our church. All day Sunday and Wednesday night were spent at church. Weekdays, school homework was the priority; watching the television was not allowed on school nights. The kids' sports events filled Saturday. I left the house at four-forty-five in the morning for work each weekday and returned home for dinner at five-thirty. I was still the absent dad at breakfast, but was indeed part of the family. Unlike in San Francisco, I was conscious when I got home from work.

The personality of the church God wanted us to attend was very different from our Marin County church. Our new church was a congregation of 7,000 people compared to 450. It is known as "the church with a heart" because its focus is reaching out to others. Getting the focus off of "you" has a life-changing effect. When we arrived in Phoenix, I clearly heard in my spirit that I was to "learn" meekness and mercy. He sent us to that church to change me. My aggressive, volatile trader personality began to soften. Altogether, we attended eighteen years, even including our five years in Albuquerque narrated later. Through the many "ministries" in which I participated, my personality moved from self-focused toward people-focused.

The long, pressurized working hours finally took a toll on my health. I wore my immune system down so much that "yuppie pneumonia" turned into "valley fever", a fungal infection common in Phoenix, that led to an extremely dangerous "cocci meningitis". I had a one in three chance of not surviving what was the only cure at that time. Until I recovered, I was to receive a bi-weekly injection of a very strong drug into the back of my neck with a three-inch-long needle to reach my spinal fluid. However, God protects His children. Through the diligent prayers of my wife, a cure was found through swallowing pills. My wife found a Gideon Bible in the emergency room waiting area, and opened it to a verse in Jeremiah 33 that says God will give you a hope and a cure. She prayed it to God and believed it would happen. That day God connected us with a doctor who did the testing for what is now a widely used anti-fungal drug. It had just become FDA approved, and my doc knew how to use it because he did the trials. The fungal infection had lodged in my spinal fluid and up on the third cranial nerve, so it was very difficult to get a drug to it. The doc gave me an extremely strong dosage in pill form. By the grace of God, the drug worked. It took four months out of my life, but, most importantly, it changed my work ethic. I was no longer addicted to the bond market twenty-four hours a day, but my personality still reflected the Bible verse quoted on page six. I was in a "dank cellar" living a "dark life!"

As described in the previous chapter, the next test for our family life was the move to Albuquerque. It did not have the miraculous provision as did the moves to San Francisco and Phoenix. The "dark life" continued in Albuquerque, compounded by the evil spiritual atmosphere. To combat the atmosphere, we attended Bible College. We studied God's Word to build up our faith to stand against the Native American and New Age influence. The years in Albuquerque were very different and difficult. My bond market career ended there. The transition to an entrepreneurial career was hard for me at first because I was no longer intensely focused. In a strange way I was visionless and empty. To the good, however, I had time at home that was great for my youngest daughter. My oldest daughter finished high school and started college, and my son was a star football tackle/linebacker in high school. They both had grown up without me, compared to the attention I was now giving my youngest. Unfortunately, that special attention to my youngest only lasted a year. The business I created eventually became just as consuming as the bond market. Our youngest daughter had an absent dad again. In later years, I repented and tried to give her the "dad" she needed.

Unless you make a conscious effort to do differently, you will raise your kids the way you were raised. Having had little experience with kids and preoccupied with job, I raised them exactly as I was raised, including having an absent dad. I was aware of my emotional deficiency and tried to overcome it. I wanted to be especially close to my oldest daughter in those early years. I took her on "dates". Oh, how I loved her. The love, however, was not exactly mutual. She had connected enough with her biological dad to feel uncomfortable accepting me completely. She grew to love me and does to this day. Yet it is not 100% acceptance. I think part of that lack of acceptance comes from the spirit of mammon. I was raised under that spirit in that we lived frugally growing up. My parents, as were many parents of baby-boomers, were strongly influenced by the effects of the Great Depression. My generation of prosperous baby-boomers doesn't live by that fear. They spend lavishly through what they think is the magic of credit. However, I was living in another world, a world of scarcity, of loss when a trade lost money. I lived in the same fear in which my parents raised me. I was controlled by it - the negative side of the spirit of mammon. In my daughter's eyes, my view of "money" stood in sharp contrast to the dads of her friends, who spent frivolously on them. She thought I didn't love her because I was tight with money. Our relationship was "mammonized". Some of those dads could have been under the control of the greed side of mammon if they thought they could buy the love of their kids with things as they worked a sixty-hour week and had little time for relationship with them. In our case, however, I was damaging the family relationships by outwardly denying them what they wanted. All they wanted was an expression that I cared for them and that I wanted to see them happy. I didn't want to deny them and I didn't see myself as doing that. I told them that I just didn't want to go into debt. Their "love language" did not understand, so they felt unloved. The spirit of mammon in me crushed them.

One thing is for sure. I have always tried to communicate to my children the message from the Bible that says that you should not compare yourself to others because you are uniquely and wonderfully made by God. Yet, I realize that from my narrow focus, I always looked through the distorted lens of my own "issues". Since money was the root "hurt" in my own heart, I got upset when a family member paid too much for an item. After all, I forecasted the inflation statistics, so I knew how much it "should" cost! Raised in that atmosphere, the three kids responded differently. The oldest saw the focus on money as denial of her wants. Now in her twelfth successful, well-paid year with a Dow Jones Industrials company, she, her husband and two kids have about anything they want. She had a dream wedding in the small German hometown of her truly wonderful husband. Our son responded to it by saying to himself that he would never allow himself to be in the attitude we lived in as a family with such an intense focus on money. He now has a very highly paid job with a Dow Jones Industrials company in San Francisco, just moved from his house on Russian Hill (now rented) to live in Marin County with his beautiful "college-sweetheart" wife and two kids. Our two oldest children both saved and worked hard to get where they are today. <u>They managed money to work for them.</u> THEY CONTROL MONEY.

Our youngest has her Mom's "right-brain" temperament. She travelled the world with Youth With A Mission out of high school, completing her college with a degree in Film (Set Design) at age 25. She is now living hand-to-mouth using her interior design talents in Southern California. She, of course, would like the comforts that money brings, but she is not as driven to get it as I was. She is a team-player hopefully with the right team and has faith that a successful career will blossom. She has the vision and the persistence to get where she wants to go. We all stand behind her.

Our three kids are now adults! We thank God that they have discovered the path that seems well for them and are growing in who they are. A delight to watch as our family grows and grows ever closer together.

Back To The Square Mile: Mammonized

Hopefully, you are now beginning to understand some of the significant issues that I have been wrestling with for the greater part of my life. There was a critical and unique moment in my story that I want to invite you to return to with me. We'll need to go back across the Atlantic "Pond" to the island that was once the very center of world trade and commerce where the God of Abraham, Isaac and Jacob had spoken so clearly into my life through a supernatural encounter. We will be returning to what I today refer to as the center of the center of the center. I liken it to the heart of the world.

My life's mammon experience comes mainly from fear and a spirit of lack. The addiction to mammon also comes out of greed. Ironically, I lived my career in the same industry that is commonly known for its extravagant lifestyle of power-hungry, self-seeking greed, Wall Street and "the City", London's financial district. The spirit of mammon expressed as greed is the same spirit that is expressed from fear and the spirit of lack, but it is in a different package. It is a motive - a controlling addiction - that distorts reality. Innate internal values of right & wrong become distorted. You can "trade your life away" through greed just as unconsciously, just as destructively, as you can through fear and lack.

Let's go back to my "Bank Circle Encounter" of July 6, 2012. Under the bright white light I heard a voice say: "you have been controlled by the same spirit that controls the City of London - the spirit of mammon. It will begin to come off of you, and as it does, it will begin to come off the City of London".

Two days after my "Bank Circle Encounter", our fifth day in London, we went to the Sunday morning service at The Commonwealth Church, pastored by Rod and Julie Anderson. I wrote in my travel diary:

> "The service began with the sound of a soft guitar. The white light and tears came over me again. I heard in my spirit God say: 'I am taking you in My Hand. We are going forward together.' Moments later Pastor Julie mentioned the spirit of mammon, referring to the pull of Harrods Department Store a few blocks away. It became clear in my spirit what God intended for me in London."

A week later we had lunch with Pastors Rod & Julie after the Sunday morning service. As I told them about the Bank Circle Encounter, tears started welling up in her eyes. She has been an intercessory prayer leader in London's Christian community and in its political arena for many years. She told me that she has been praying against the spirit of mammon in London for years and that she "knew" that I was sent to London with an "apostolic mantle". Because of my twenty-year career trading bonds and my experience dealing with the spirit of mammon, she told me that God has now called me to oppose and expose that very spirit.

It is the intent of this book to expose the spirit of mammon. I am walking hand-in-hand with God to oppose it. Because it is an evil spirit, it must be opposed in the spirit.

As I said earlier, our YWAM Megacities assignment was to prayer walk the "Square Mile" portion of the "City" of London and work with the churches there to create unity. As a result of my Bank Circle encounter, my prayer burden assignment was obviously battling the spirit of mammon in The City. Over the ensuing two weeks, I walked and prayed over every block of the Square Mile.

I was greeted every time we left our church building by the symbolic mascot of the City of London, Gog and Magog, one of which is carved in an overpass railing a short distance from our church home toward St. Paul's Cathedral. It is evil. The first time I saw it, my spirit closed and I walked away from it. As I walked every block of the Square Mile, I saw it repeatedly and am embarrassed to say that I got used to it. It is an evil image and an accurate representation of the spiritual climate in the City. We prayed that its power would be broken, for I believe that is one of the "places" the spirit of mammon resides. I had a similar reaction to the Freemasons' Hall (the Masonic Temple headquarters), which is between where we lived and Covent Gardens. I literally had to turn away from it as well. It is a very evil place and another "home" to the spirit of mammon. My Bank Circle encounter had made me sensitive to the presence of the spirit of mammon and created a desire in my spirit to turn from it.

As my prayer walking continued, I began to see and feel the history of London, specifically the Square Mile. For over two hundred years, the British Empire was the heartbeat of a world-wide empire of commerce over the seas, financed by the prominent members of the Masonic Temple and the leadership of the Square Mile. Their focus was mammon. Power-mongering and greed were the rule of the day. They were so elite that even the Queen had to be invited "in". Their focus on wealth and power caused them to exclude God.

When the British defeated the Turks in 1917, England was given control of much of what is now the Middle East. They turned their back on God when they gave away to the Arabs what is now Jordan, which should have been the land of Israel. It can be said that God turned His back on the British Empire because it gave away His "land". That was the final blow to an Empire that was already waning. At the same, with God still at the foundation of its democracy, America began to emerge as the world power.

Today, the City is the center of investment securities trading which, because of its history, lacks the regulatory oversight found in other financial centers. It is outside the governmental jurisdiction of the British Parliament. It has its own government & policing authority controlled politically by the financial institutions and the Church of England. It is a playground for greed. However, since my Bank Circle encounter, God has caused changes, as He promised. Much of the corruption within the banking industry has been exposed since July 6, 2012. Parliament is involved. Furthermore, in 2014 a new Archbishop of Canterbury was named to head the Church of England, a major influence in the politics of the City. He comes from the business interests of the City, but he is working to change the ethic of the City out of its greed mentality. God has begun the process of removing the spirit of mammon.

The City of London is a city and a ceremonial center within London. It is a city within a city and often referred to simply as the City and even written simply as "City". Also, one may refer to it as the Square Mile as it is a mere 1.12 square mile (2.90km). Both names represent the United Kingdom's financial services industry and have long been the central base for trade throughout the notable history of the British Empire. The name London has long been used for the far greater surrounding area, out beyond the City of London. London, the Greater London administrative area, is made up of 32 boroughs, including the City of Westminster, where Parliament is located, in addition to the City of London itself.

The City of London constituted most of London from its settlement by the Romans in the 1st century AD to the Middle Ages. The City is now only a tiny part of the metropolis of London, yet a notable part of busy central London. It is governed by the City of London Corporation with responsibilities for a local council and the police authority. It was outside the jurisdiction of Parliament and, therefore, became a center for insatiable greed. The Corporation is headed by the Lord Mayor of the City of London, an office separate from (and much older than) The Mayor of London. The financial institutions and the Church of England control its politic. The City of London can be considered the most important city in England, Great Britain, and today's United Kingdom, as well as yesterday's great British Empire...on whom the sun has now set. In the 19th century, the Square Mile was the world's primary business and financial center and continues today as a major meeting point for global finance, especially trading.

There is no place quite like The City. Not only is it the oldest section of London with an amazing history, it is the world's leading international financial and business center with over 300,000 workers and less than 10,000 residents. The City also has its own unique system of administration and is not classified as a "borough", but rather is a small "district" at the heart of London.

Established around AD50, seven years after the Romans invaded Britain, the Square Mile as it has become known, is the very place from which modern-day London grew. The remains of the City's Roman wall can still be seen in various locations, yet it's not just the Roman remains and medieval structures that make the City's buildings so unique. The modern contemporary architecture designed to house today's global business giants that are located here sit side by side with the history's ancient past. The Romans called the place Londinium and knew it was ideally located for business. Situated on the north bank of the River Thames, it soon became a bustling port and trade thrived. As business increased, tradesmen came together to form livery companies or 'guilds' to regulate trade. Milk Street, Bread Street, Ironmonger Lane, Poultry, Cloth Fair, and Mason's Avenue mark the sites where those companies began.

These guilds would soon come to yield great power and influence as London developed a reputation as a center for European trade. By the early 17th century as the age of exploration began in the world, totally new markets developed many guilds that invested money in setting up merchant venture companies. The most famous of these companies was the East India Company, which would find exclusive rights for trade. Their unique power lasted until well into the 19th century.

During the 19th century, London became the first "world city" with a growing population distributed over a very large geographical area. As a world city, London attracted the dispossessed and ambitious from all four corners of the world, as well as the poor and the politically oppressed from southern and eastern Europe. Immigrants arrived from British possessions throughout the world, particularly India and China. It was the center of world trade.

London was the capital of Great Britain, the capital of the British Empire, and the capital of the British Commonwealth of Nations. Its naval power would guarantee England the head seat at the table of world affairs. Like other capital cities, London was a political and administrative center, with vested civil servants in expanding bureaucracies and ambitious political figures. But, most important of all, it was also the financial center, the hub of the rail and road system, and a large marketplace for goods and services. The City Center now housed government buildings and mercantile activities. It is also destined to be the cultural center of the Empire. Newspaper and book publishers flourished, as well as theaters and operas, restaurants, and a variety of small gardens of 19th century pleasure.

London, amongst the oldest of Europe's capital cities, was Europe's largest urban community and, in the 19th century was England's only large city. Her size and wealth had been a factor in the growth of the English economy, needing coal, food, wood and wheat. From around 1700, London was Europe's and the world's greatest port and commercial center, a role London would retain until the 20th century. It was to be the administrative and financial center of a kingdom, The British Empire. And, there, at the very center of the great city was The City...its very heart...its very core.

So, what was it that God was showing me...was now asking of me.... that fateful, rainy July day in 2012...there I was frozen in time, at the very heart of that still proud city. What did it all mean? There I stood, from hand to foot frozen into God's indescribable moment of timelessness. I knew that I was about to under-go a dramatic change. As though God was adding profundity to profundity, I heard that this ancient Square Mile would begin to change, as well. Somehow, this bruised n' battered trader's heart of mine was now connected to the great and worldly financial heart of the nations. 'My God', I thought...'how could this possibly be'?

Then, no sooner than I had thought the thought, when suddenly I understood. It was my heart. God had brought me here because He wanted to show me, as only a loving Father could say to one of His beloved children... "Son, I want you to change". You see, I had arrived in London wearing YWAM-fashioned missionary footwear. However, the God of Creation, the very one that told the prophet Jeremiah that "Before I formed you in the womb, I knew you," was about to impart in me a message to take to the nations of the earth. I had thought that I was coming to fulfill a "call" to YWAM. I had not considered that He was the One bringing me specifically to London for "such a time as this". Once more, my Father God was giving, but what was the gift He was offering? Simply, it was and still is, "understanding" of the call He has for me. He wanted my eyes to be opened and He wanted my ears to be able to hear and He wanted to continue schooling me in His ways. There was ever so much of me, of my heart, that He wanted to continue to fashion into the image of His Son Jesus. He wanted me to be more and more like Jesus and less and less like the worldly man that I had, over a lifetime, become. So, was I a born again believer? Yes, most certainly. With His promised salvation? Yes, again, most certainly. But, you see, there was so much more of me that needed, and still needs, to change.

But, why had He chosen one of this world's most unique places for my encounter? Why there? Remember that He had spoken so clearly to me: "You have been controlled by the same spirit that controls the City of London - the spirit of mammon. It will begin to come off of you, and, as it does, it will begin to come off the City of London". There were so very many questions.

My purpose became somewhat more directed when I returned home to read that Barclays Bank, one of the largest banks headquartered in The City, had just confessed to illegally rigging the LIBOR rate on which thousands of home mortgages are priced today around the world. Within weeks God had begun the process of peeling off the power of the spirit of mammon in London.

I had a consuming career on or trading with Wall Street where greed was and is the rule of the day. The spirit of mammon is still today controlling the souls of Wall Street. But my catharsis didn't happen on Wall Street; the life-changing event happened to me in the Square Mile.

Why London? The spirit of mammon - the root that drives Wall Street - can be traced to the Square Mile. The Royal Stock Exchange, the first in the City, opened in 1571, as a center of commerce. The site was provided by the Corporation of the City of London and the Worshipful of Mercers. However, traders too rowdy for the

Exchange gathered at Jonathan's Coffee-House in 1695. Other coffee houses soon followed and eventually became the London Stock Exchange. The 24 traders who met at Jonathan's were a secretive and exclusive group, meeting at a time when the trading of commodities was established. In the eighteenth and nineteenth centuries, as Britain's global dominance on the sea was expanded and solidified, massive world-wide trade routes brought the need for the British Empire to be financed. The City became the wealth-springs that gave life to the flourishing high-seas dominant Empire. The success of trading commodities created a global trail of greed as the price for a homogenous product with limited supply goes through various stages of markup. The City financed the growth of the nineteenth century Empire. As the British economic influence began to wane early in the twentieth century, America's influence began its meteoric rise to prominence. The tree of Wall Street grew out of the roots of the British Empire. A spiritual "root" of greed and corruption was transferred and it is still part of the root structure today. Greed and corruption are at the heart of the global financial community.

My Bank Circle experience must personally be considered a spiritual catharsis. My squinty-eyed life of fear and lack had to be supernaturally opened to a life of peace. I had to be separated from the spirit of mammon. A "root" found in the Square Mile had to be severed at its source. I needed the warm touch of God to melt the cold reality of the financial world at its root. Both my mind and spirit had been opened by traveling across Europe the month before, leaving me as much a blank tablet as I could be when we arrived in London. God could now impregnate me with the vision and power of the calling for which I had been waiting many years. I finally reached the experiential maturity to walk in the authority God had given me. The Bank Circle Encounter gave me that authority, a mantle to expose and oppose the spirit of mammon at its root where it is strongest- the Square Mile "City".

A Warning from God:
MICAH 6:8-14
The Message Bible

"But he's [God] already made it clear how to live, what to do, what God is looking for in men and women. It is quite simple: Do what is fair and just to your neighbor, be compassionate and loyal in your love, and don't take yourself too seriously - take God seriously.

Attention! God calls out to the City! If you know what's good for you, you'll listen. So listen, all of you! This is serious business. Do you expect me [God] to overlook obscene wealth you've piled up by cheating and fraud? Do you think I'll tolerate shady deals and shifty scheming? I'm tired of the violent rich bullying their way with bluffs and lies. I'm fed up. Beginning now, you're finished. You'll pay for your sins down to your last cent. No matter how much you get, it will never be enough - hollow stomachs, empty hearts. No matter how hard you work, you'll have nothing to show for it - bankrupt lives, wasted souls."

Free From the Spirit
of Mammon

Detoxing the Spirit of Mammon - A Scientific Solution

"as a man thinks, so is he" Proverbs 23:7

We will achieve freedom from the spirit of mammon from two sources - the mind and the heart. We will explore your thought life to get to your mind and then develop your spiritual life to get to your heart. You will have a framework for change.

We begin by using scientific research to examine and change your thought life. Current research has developed the science of neuroplasticity. It has been discovered that you can learn how to accept or reject negative toxic thoughts that you are thinking in your mind before they get to your brain and become who you are. You control your brain through your thoughts and choices. The implications are enormous as we will discover. As you have seen in my life story, I have been under the control of a negative toxic spirit, the spirit of mammon. For over thirty years, I have been unable to completely come out from under its control. We will now use the research and practice of Dr. Carolyn Leaf to scientifically destroy the power of the spirit of mammon over my - and your - personality. I strongly encourage you to read her book from which most of the material of this chapter originates, <u>Switch on Your Brain, The Key to Peak Happiness, Thinking and Health</u>.

the basics - how your thought life works

Dr. Leaf says that being who we are is where happiness lies, but that this is most often blocked by who we have become. As a communication pathologist specializing in cognitive neuroscience, she has studied intensively how humans think and how that affects what they say and do. Her research in the 1990's concluded that the unconscious mind is much more powerful than the conscious mind and that "when you engage the unconscious mind through deep thinking, you bring memories into the conscious mind in a vulnerable state, which means you can change them - or reconceptualize them. Through your thinking, you can actively recreate your thoughts and, therefore, knowledge in your brain."[3] This is the key to changing your thought life. You can't control the circumstances that hit you, but you can control your reaction to those circumstances, and you have the ability to choose your reaction. That reaction begins as a thought in your mind.

The scientific discipline of quantum physics says that _you_ control the choices you make. Your brain is directed by that on which you focus. Your brain controls what you say and do by the attention you give to your thoughts and feelings. Dr. Leaf gives the following example:

1. Information: you get a call from your doctor's office telling you that the results of your blood test are in and asks you to phone them as soon as possible.
2. Thoughts: Multiple thoughts are swirling around in your head. Option one is fear: "They said as soon as possible! Does that mean bad news? What if I have..." And on it goes, down to planning the songs for your funeral. Option two is denial: "This is routine; I'll call when I have time." Option

---

3   Dr. Caroline Leaf, <u>Switch on Your Brain</u>, The Key to Peak, Thinking, and Health (Grand Rapids, MI, Baker Books, 2013) p 141.

three is trust: "I have faith that this will be good news. I am
not moved by any doctor's report."

3. Choice: You choose an option. For instance, if you choose
    fear, your brain responds by wiring in the thought, "I am
    sick," and you live into this thought.
4. Consequence: You suddenly feel sick and are sure you are
    dying.
5. New consequence: You phone the doctor; your results show
    nothing wrong; and you suddenly feel fine (and perhaps a
    little foolish).

This happens to all of us more than we are willing to admit. As you
can see from this example, the thought we choose has a powerful
creative force. Examine your thoughts and take them seriously.

Dr. Leaf has created a model to illustrate how a thought becomes
a memory that influences behavior. Information from the external
world outside of our mind comes into our conscious mind through
our five senses. An emotional response is immediately activated.
To be in control of our thought life, we should try to process and
evaluate that emotion at that point. Unfortunately, we usually let
it slip past. The information then passes into the unconscious level
of our mind where ninety percent of the mind's activity occurs. If
you respond to the thought in this subconscious level, it becomes a
physical thought through the making of proteins and can complete
the cycle by impacting your conscious mind and, then, your senses.
The more a thought repeats this cycle, the stronger it grows. After
twenty-one days of cycling back and forth, enough protein changes
have occurred to create a standing memory. You must continue
nurturing that thought for twenty-one days to affect change. If you
stop prematurely, the memory dies and becomes heat energy. If you
repeat the twenty-one day cycle three times, it becomes a habit firmly
implanted in your brain..

We see the world through the thoughts (memories) we have built into our brains. Those thoughts/memories are made through our choices. Dr. Lief says the brain is a photocopy machine for thoughts solidified in our mind. She says that "the way you experience your feelings, the way you interface with your thoughts, and the kind of attention you give them will change how your brain functions." So our mind (subconscious and conscious) is separate from our brain. In fact, your mind controls your brain through the thoughts that complete the 21-day cycle. When we complete three 21-day cycles, we create a long-term memory or habit. We can change the way we see the world, and as a consequence who we are, by being disciplined in controlling the thoughts that securely enter the brain.

the how to - 5 steps to taking charge of and changing your thought life

Dr. Leaf created five steps to "switch on your brain". She says "in essence what you will be doing with the 5 steps is bringing the toxic thought into the conscious mind and then proceeding, over 21 days, to destroy it. Mind controls matter. At the same time, you will be growing a healthy new thought to replace the toxic one, so you will be consciously and simultaneously building up healthy thoughts and tearing down toxic thoughts. You work on only one thought network each 21-day cycle." Your brain responds to the thoughts of your mind through the five steps below. Do the first four steps each day, taking a few minutes for each step. Step five - the action step - should be done several times a day.

Step 1: Become aware of your thoughts - discern what is already in your mind (memories) and what is trying to come into your mind from the external environment through your five senses.

You are beginning the process of bringing your thoughts into captivity by developing an awareness of what you are experiencing from your senses through your thoughts. You are becoming aware of your thoughts so they can be tested. It is not until you bring a subconscious thought into consciousness that you "feel" the emotion that is always attached to the thought subconsciously. An attitude then develops from that thought feeling. A positive attitude results in a peaceful feeling and a stressful feeling results from a negative attitude.

Dr. Leaf suggests that you ask yourself the following questions to become aware of your thoughts:

What are you experiencing through your five senses as you read this? Become aware of what is coming into your mind.
What thoughts are coming to you at this moment? Focus on how many and what they are.
What is the attitude and feeling of those thoughts?
Do the thoughts make you feel peace or worry?
Do you feel victorious or a victim?
Do you feel dominated by the thought feeling?
Can you feel a stress reaction in your body?
Do I want that thought to be part of me?

Step 2: Focus and reflect on a negative thought with the intent to change it.

According to Dr. Lief, brain scans show that the areas of the brain activated by an action are similarly activated by simply thinking about the action. Get alone without distraction. Get your mind in a quiet place. Connect your mind to what is deep inside you in your spirit. You are in an introspective state. You are in a state of rest. Now catch your thoughts. Dr. Lief says that "through modifying our practices of thought toward a more disciplined, focused, and reflective thought life, we can build up healthy neural real estate that is better able to bring our thoughts into captivity and deal with the variegated demands of today's modern world."

Step 3: Write down the "pattern" of the thought to better define and add clarity to what you have been thinking about. Write down the different circumstances in which the thought occurs and what causes the thought in those circumstances. Write down the different emotions involved in those circumstances. Write down the details as they come to you. Start with the basic thought and get into its nuances. Start with the general "feeling" and get to the thought. Is there a sequence or repetitiveness? What are your internal responses in each? By writing this down on paper, you are looking to see the interaction of the conscious and unconscious thoughts. You are defining a thought pattern that can be detoxed in the next two steps. Keep a journal of your thoughts.

Step 4: Evaluate the negative thought in the light of what you have written down and create a positive thought to replace it. Dr. Leaf observes that "when thoughts are activated and pushed into the conscious mind, they enter a labile state - meaning they can be altered. When a memory is in this "plastic" state, it can be modified, toned down, or retranscribed by interfering with protein synthesis - an important molecular process in thought building." If you mentally focus intensely on a thought to the point of actually rehearsing it, you can build a new memory thought. The more you do it, the stronger the new memory, both negative and positive. You can destroy negative thoughts (strongholds) by bringing the thought into conscious awareness and change it through a commitment to not do it again and through forgiveness of yourself and/or others. This causes a chemical change (protein synthesis) in your brain, allowing you to replace the negative thought with a positive thought. Evaluate the negativity in the thought and change it to a positive thought. It may take several days. Think deep introspection. Plant the positive thought. It evolves and grows over the 21 days of doing step five. You are detoxing the thought.

Step 5: Repeat the new positive thought with action. Reach beyond where you are. You do something with the detoxing. It is not the decision - it is the doing. This step is a continuing action on the thought. Say and do the new thought <u>several times a day</u> for one 21 day cycle. Then, to make it a habit, speak and do it for two more 21 day cycles.

what is happening? - as a man thinks, so is he

The awareness step helps creates discipline to watch what is going in and coming out of your mind so that no thought controls you. I am taking charge of my thought life and, as a result, becoming responsible for who I am. As I began the introspective hunt for negative mammon thoughts, I became acutely aware of how negative my thought life had become. My self-talk revealed that I don't like "me" and my low-self esteem inhibits my relationship with other people, especially men. I hide who I really am in a huge false pride.

The awareness step was difficult for me. I was breaking through a habitual way of thinking that doesn't want to change. Distractions and excuses were never ending. Because I was dealing with the subconscious as well as the conscious, the spiritual battle was intense. After all, I was attacking a strong evil spirit (the love of money) that has had a grip on me for most of my adult life though the emotion of fear. The thought "what if?" seems to become emotionalized at my conscious level of thinking. My brain then creates a response that acts to stabilize the emotion that is tied to that thought. I respond with an emotional decision out of fear instead of out of rational thinking. I have found that that type of thinking is responsible for most losing trades in my market trading over the last thirty-five years.

Let's go back in my life story. I relinquished control over my trading to a fear. I thought that my futures trades were being monitored. I thought trading losses were forced upon me (victim mentality?) by a powerful trader. As the thought pattern continued, it became habitually implanted on my brain. I even began to anticipate and expect the trading loss to occur. The fear - the spirit of mammon - was in control. Instead of changing the thought pattern, both subconscious and conscious, I reinforced the fear by trying to create ways to outsmart its presence. I changed the company with whom I traded. I tried tweaking my trading system, or changing account numbers & passwords, or placing the order a different way. In 2007 I even wrote a letter to the Sr VP in charge of security for the firm I traded with detailing all the security breaches. In 2010, I wrote a letter to the CFTC (futures market regulatory authority) and contacted the FBI because I was a victim of the equity markets's "flash crash". I was making the fear "thought" even more real by responding to it rather than replacing it. I had been doing that for thirty years. I was a proven victim!

The fear emotion, however, is prevalent in my general thought life as well as in the trading decisions. Through the years of trading, my personality deteriorated to a fear that I would not be able to meet my financial obligations and provide for my family, the fear side of the spirit of mammon. It had such a hold on me that it became "me". I thought that I had no alternative but to keep trading. In a recently published book, Who Is Behind The Mask?[4], Dr. Allen McCray describes what I think my personality had become. He would call it a combination "C/S" personality where I am growing down rather than up. The spiral down begins with the anxiety that I cannot pay the bills if I don't make enough on a trade or if I lose money on a trade, which "leads to anxiousness, pessimism, and suspiciousness, which cause internal conflict that vacillates between impulsiveness, caution, and indecision. This downward movement may cause a reactive behavior that increases feelings of insecurity and leaves the

---

[4]   Allen McCray, Who's Behind the Mask? Become Who You Have Always Been but Were Never Allowed to Be (Bloomington, IN, iUniverse LLC, 2014),p125.

C/S types feeling panicky, depressed, and helpless. They can harbor paranoid fears and delusional ideas about the world. They may rant about their obsessive fears and strike out at real or imagined enemies. (Do you see that in me? Try the previous paragraph!) C/S personality types can grow up (and out of it) by letting go of the belief that they must rely on (or be victim to) someone or something outside themselves for support, and instead discover their own inner guidance. The growth process is reinforced when they grow a healthy self-image by forming alliances with others and building connections through stability, dependability, and trustworthiness." That inner guidance for me has become the "silent" voice of the Holy Spirit as I spend more time with God.

I encourage you to read Dr. McCray's book to help you discover your personality and what life's events can do to it.

It is now easy to see an objective way to get rid of the spirit of mammon - change my thinking. As a man thinks, so is he. This chapter suggests a scientific approach - neuroplasticity and the interaction of personality traits - to change behavior using a defined methodology. Unfortunately, the spirit of mammon is more than just behavior and getting out from under its control is more than just behavior modification. It is a spiritual battle that must be fought in the heart and spirit as well as the brain. My "step five" of Dr. Lief's "5-step brain detox plan" is to walk out of the victim mentality that leaves me helpless. I began to take charge of my thought life by observing and replacing the negative thoughts that enter my brain and, as a result, fear began to lessen. Yet I had an identity crisis. I could not really come to grips with who I am and what my life would be without fear and the spirit of lack. There was no peace and contentment. The spirit of mammon had consumed my soul. As my brain detoxes and my personal self-talk becomes stronger and more positive, I walk along the road of faith with my God-given destiny in sight. Get ready, get ready - I am about to walk into peace and contentment.

How To Walk The "Faith Road":
Man Does Not Live By Bread Alone,
But By Every Word That Comes
Out Of The Mouth Of God

In God's eyes, man is not to live for himself by himself and do his own selfish thing. Man is called to a higher purpose – a purpose put in each one of us before we were born. True inner peace and contentment can only come through that purpose. The Biblical book of Jonah is the story of a man, Jonah, refusing to accept a God-given purpose or "call". I described in "Finding the Faith Road" above how my life changed when I met Jesus. My spiritual nature awakened. Each of us is born with a spiritual nature and purpose, but it lies in the background of our consciousness. We must purposely and publicly unlock it. I found my spiritual nature and unlocked it with a sincere change of focus and priority. Unfortunately, for thirty years, I couldn't shake off the spirit of mammon, a demonic spirit that wanted to and succeeded in stealing my life's purpose, my peace and contentment. I had awakened my spiritual nature, but not my purpose. When you have found your God-given purpose and walk in it, you have found peace and contentment. I wasn't there yet. The spirit of mammon kept me distracted chasing a goal - money - that it would not let me reach.

Man's spiritual purpose can be reached in many different ways, but we must take the initiative to reach it. The essential element is faith that believes that the spiritual realm exists and influences our soul (mind, will, and emotions). As we relinquish control of our soul to God, we receive His love in our spirit and are, then, on the road to finding peace and contentment. We can't make ourselves be content and full of peace. We need help, and God will help us as we ask Him.

Get into the spiritual realm and get supernatural help. Because the spiritual nature resides in your heart rather than your head, you can't "think" it from your brain. You must be in relationship with God. He will reside in your heart when you let Him into it. Once He is there, He becomes the source of your knowledge - not head knowledge, but heart knowledge. You learn to speak and do from your heart through His nudgings.

Finding your spiritual purpose requires letting go of the negatives of your past. It is a necessary spiritual journey of forgiving yourself for your failures, but you can't effectively command forgiveness. This comes from the heart, not the head. Forgiveness requires a heart change. With that heart change, a new head perspective emerges with a new direction, which is based on your spiritual nature. The longest road in life is getting from your head to your heart. I suggest below a relatively simple way to travel down that road. It worked for me and it can work for you!

In my life as a bond trader, I was <u>proud</u> of MY ability to forecast the market. My identity was a head thing. I recognized that Wall Street deliberately forecasted economic statistics erroneously because it made <u>them</u> money when traders/investors lost money following their advice. I suffered from a near-paranoia lack of trust in the financial markets that spread to all areas of my life. My only source of faith, the only "voice" I trusted, was "me". That intense kind of self-centered focus is not healthy. It leads to a dependence on perfectionism that no one can obtain. Reread the Matthew 6:21-23 quote at the beginning of this book. I was squinty-eyed in greed and distrust, living a dark life.

No man should be alone as an island unto himself and I was an island. When I awakened that morning in 1982 asking 'is this all there is' to life, I found the way off my island and onto that road from my head to my heart. Here's how that happened.

It was a hot Sacramento Monday in early July, 1982. I ran my daily jog home from the office, took a shower, ate a sandwich, and went to a social gathering of several hundred single men and women. I went for the expressed purpose of breaking out of the personal prison cell I had lived in for many years. Deep inside I was desperately looking for intimacy. Outwardly, I hoped to meet a lady who would change my life, but I didn't know what to expect.

Well, it was a supernatural experience! I sat in one of about fifteen hundred theatre-style seats. A five-member band began a soft, melodic Peter, Paul & Mary-type folksy song that quieted my mind. Then another, then another. I was captivated. Tears began streaming down my cheeks. I didn't understand what had happened, but I was suddenly stress-free and at peace. I was not aware of anybody or anything. A supernatural relationship was unknowingly initiated. Jesus Christ began touching my heart. I didn't understand at the time that He was waiting for me to acknowledge Him so the relationship - an intimate spiritual relationship - could be established. It took me some time to turn off my inquiring mind so I could understand in my spirit that Jesus was knocking at the door of my heart. Suddenly, my spirit had ears to hear.

A few weeks later I attended a Bible study. Before a group of guys (one of whom was the Singles Group drummer), I prayed with clarity of voice and love in my heart that "I receive Jesus Christ as my Lord and Savior. I confess that I am a sinner living in a selfish, miserably lonely life and I repent of my previous life choices and of my sins. Jesus died on the cross and rose from the dead to save me from the miserably lonely life that I am living as I surrender to Him and accept Him as my Lord and Savior." At that moment His love overwhelmed me. I became a child of God able to receive the love of God. He now resides in my heart. I was stepping off the island of self! I was beginning the journey down the long road from my head to my heart.

Anyone speaking those words and believing them in his/her heart can step off their island as well. Say it out loud right now where you are and receive His love and acceptance.

I am now a child of God, a "believer" in God and His love for me. His supernatural love conquers all. I was still in the mammon-centered world, but I had a new hope. I would need to develop my "spirit" man so it can lead me. Roman 12:2 in the New Living Translation says: "Don't copy the world, but let God transform you into a new person by changing the way you think. Then you will know what God wants you to do, and you will know how good and pleasing His perfect will really is." You change, or rather, God changes the way you think by seeing the world around you (your job, your relationships, even yourself) through the eyes of your spirit. You awakened the eyes of your spirit when you said "yes" to Jesus. He will save you from the material world of mammon as you develop your spirit by reading God's instruction manual, the Bible. This is a crucial step that you must undertake to overcome the spirit of mammon.

You will know His expectations of you as you read the Bible. Begin by reading the New Testament. Devour it. As a Christian we are to become Christ-like. In Matthew, Mark, Luke, and John, be sensitive to the character of Jesus. For example, identify with His love, His compassion, His gentleness, His patience, His servanthood, and His humility.

In time you will have a believing, trusting personal relationship with God. You will hear His voice through a conviction in your spirit. He will nudge you in your spirit to do or not do something. Be obedient to the nudge. However, you must know what the Bible says. He will NEVER tell you something that contradicts what the Bible says. Be discerning.

We can get out of God's will - what the Bible says we should say or do or be - by doing our own thing. He gives us free will. He lets us do what we want so that we can live the adverse consequences of what we do out of our own desires, rather than choosing His will. We will eventually see the wisdom of His ways. However, we are not blessed by God when we are doing something obviously out of His will. On the other hand, when we are in the center of His will, we receive peace and contentment in addition to the material rewards that confirm His blessing.

Most of us live a life of selfishness based on a desire to do our own thing. It is difficult to give the decisions of our life, even the little details, to the leadership of the spiritual realm within us. However, if we have developed relationships with God the Father, Jesus His Son, and the Holy Spirit, then we can trust that "all things work together for our good". If we let the mind, will, and emotions of the human side of us control the spiritual side (which is the case most of the time, for most of us), then we will probably not be in the perfect will of God. Fortunately, through His grace, if we acknowledge to Him that we stepped out of His will, repent (be determined not to do it again), and ask Him for forgiveness, He will forgive us and it will be forgotten - unless, of course, we do it again. But even then, if we ask for forgiveness and repent once more. He will forgive us again because He knows we are human. The blessings, the peace and contentment, come when we don't have to repeatedly ask for His forgiveness. We are then obedient to His will.

We must also be in rest. Trusting God to meet our needs creates the basis for rest, but to have sustained rest requires discipline. We must consciously eliminate negative emotions, such as fear, anger, frustration, etc. by letting go of "issues" in our life that cause those emotions and trust God to work it out. Issues are unmet needs. Trust God to meet the need. We then have the peace that God promises us, the peace that passes all understanding. We are then resting in God's will.

Walking out of the spirit of mammon requires the supernatural power of the Holy Spirit working in us to overcome the demonic spiritual realm. The Bible tells us that after you are "born again" into the Kingdom of God, the prayer you spoke from your heart above, you must then receive the power of the Holy Spirit that empowers you to do what the disciples did in the Book of Acts (specifically Acts 2:2). We must specifically ask for that power by asking in prayer to receive the baptism of the Holy Spirit and receive His power with evidence of speaking in tongues. If you believe for it in faith just like you did above, then you will receive it. Your spirit will then be empowered to communicate in the spiritual realm, often in an unknown language where your tongue will be supernaturally controlled as you speak. You then have the power to do the works of Christ, which includes commanding evil spirits, like the spirit of mammon, to leave people who are willing to let it happen, including yourself. To be in the position to walk in that power, however, you must have the mind of Christ, which comes from knowing Him and living the way the Bible says to live.

We must be devoid of self. We cannot be focusing on our own personal needs and wants, our own weaknesses and inadequacies. The only way we can be devoid of self is through the spiritual help of the Holy Spirit, who lives inside of us in our heart when we are "born again". You can't command yourself to change. Through prayer we must humbly admit to the bad habits in our lives that are in opposition to the way the Bible teaches us to live and be determined to change. We ask the Holy Spirit to work inside our inner being, our heart, to change our thought life and behavior. We need to ask the Holy Spirit to take charge continually. As the Holy Spirit convicts us in our spirit of our bad habits and we accept that "correction" and repent, we become more Christ-like.

As we consciously yield to the Holy Spirit and read the Bible daily, over time our spirit will line up with His spirit. We become confident in who we are as part of the Kingdom of God and can keep our focus there and become empowered. We are being made into the image of Jesus Christ with His power and His authority. Our assignment is to use the powers of heaven to bring the presence of heaven to the world around us. In the next chapter, it is suggested how you can walk out of the spirit of mammon by walking into the life of giving. Personally, I hope to reach the people of the City of London with this story and give them encouragement that God can take them, as He did me, away from the spirit of mammon. As I walk into that calling, I believe that supernatural power and authority will be manifested that will bring heaven to London - as promised to me at "Bank Circle" July 6, 2012.

I have been battling with evil spirits for over thirty years. They are supernatural manifestations from the pit of hell that have tried to prevent me from living Romans 12:2 quoted above. Only now am I seeing the schemes of the devil that have kept me enslaved. For example, I have never been able to read the Bible for more than half an hour without falling asleep. When I read a few verses out loud to someone, I will yawn. That has been happening uncontrollably for years. I graduated from Bible College in 1995 more from my carnal, worldly mind than from my spirit. I say this not to discourage you.

Instead, I want to encourage you to overcome the resistance that will, indeed, be there if you really want to complete the task of developing your spiritual mind. The cares of the world will try to distract you, even deceive you, as has happened to me. Satan, the god of the world, will use deception to keep you in his control. So, be persistent in getting the word of God into your spirit. This is a matter of life or death!

For thirty years I had not read the Bible as diligently as I should. Furthermore, the amount of time I spent in prayer was only minimal. The time that I did spend in verbal relationship with God was not lovingly sincere and focused. It was not the Father and son relationship that it must be. As you read above in "Mammonized Family - Redeemed", I had a distant father-son relationship with my Dad. It is difficult for me to give and receive the love of a "father". As a result, I had difficulty connecting with God heart-to-heart. Yes, I had faith to believe that He heard my prayers (requests) and would answer them, but my prayers were not sincere because they were not coming from my heart out of a loving relationship with my "Father". They were mechanical rather than relational. I was not in childlike dependence on my Heavenly Father to free me from evil spiritual manifestations. We had not been walking hand-in-hand through the situation, conversing throughout the day, day after day, trusting each other. For much of the last fifteen years or so, I didn't have that close relationship with God until we traveled across Europe with YWAM in June 2012. At that time I was free of the distractions at home, so that I could begin to walk hand-in-hand with my Heavenly Father. I found the love of and for God that I once had.

The necessity to read the word of God daily never ends. Our goal is be obedient to what the Bible requires of us, which is why we must consistently read it. It is our code of behavior. The more we live biblically and maintain a personal relationship with Jesus, the more our spirit is refilled with His power. Yet, there is an obvious next step. The power that God's Word brings to our spirit must then be transformed into action. We walk in the spirit. We do what the spirit says to do. Based on the presence of God's Word in our spirit, we are convicted to do "something". When you "hear" it, DO IT.

My wife and I have led a ministry at our church called "treasure-hunting". In a group of three or four, we ask God to tell us who He wants us to speak to and what He wants us to say. We are obedient to go where He says. For example, He told us to go to a particular store, wait where they sell watermelons and tell a lady buying a watermelon that her sister's surgery three days later will go well - don't be fearful. We wrote it down, but questioned whether we heard right because nobody has watermelons in December. We went anyway and the store He told us to go to had watermelons. We waited until a lady stepped up to look at watermelons and handed her the message God had for her. She started crying because her sister was having surgery three days later. We were obedient to deliver God's message. The more we develop our spirit to "live" in God's Word, the more we will hear God. The more we act on what we hear from God, the more we will be like God. This is our goal as a Christian. However, a word of caution. God will not tell you to say something negative or critical to anyone. If it is not positive or uplifting, it is not from God. You must develop this "gift" by having a close relationship with God, which is developed over time.

With the Word of God in you, you sail off the island of self. You are in a spiritual sea sailing on a luxury yacht. However, it is a long, long journey. My marriage of now thirty years - a "marriage made in heaven" - has been one of many storms. Becoming a Christian doesn't take away the storms of life; it gives you the ability through faith in God to make it through the storms. It is the many storms that grow you spiritually into God's character. The Bible verse from the Book of Matthew quoted as the title of this chapter describes the life on God's yacht: "Man does not live by bread alone, but by every word that comes out of the mouth of God." We worry, strive, plan, and in many other ways focus on providing the bread for our family. We are all trying to feed something - our senses, lusts, habits, stress, whatever. Instead, try feeding your spirit with the Word of God. The Bible says in the Book of Matthew that you should not "worry about having enough food or drink or clothing. Why be like the pagans who are so deeply concerned about these things? Your Heavenly Father already knows all your needs, and He will give you all you need from day to day <u>if you live for Him and make the Kingdom of God your primary concern.</u> "(New Living Translation, my emphasis)

We must trust what God promises us in the Bible, understanding that the promises are many times conditional upon something we must do. At the same time, the Bible says that He will not let the circumstance get beyond what we can handle. He simply wants us to be dependent upon Him - to let go and let God. We must be engaged in relationship with Him and His Word to know what He expects of us, and, in turn, receive His best for us. We must feed on Jesus. We must "break bread" with Him. The Bible is the bread of life. It is the word of God that we must "eat" to benefit from His full & best provision for us. We must diligently read the Bible daily, but not as you read any other book. You must read it with your spirit by beginning your time of reading in prayer, asking the Holy Spirit to give you "revelation" as you read. When you do this, you will learn that the Bible is "hope food" from God. For example, recently in prayer God said to me that when I finish this book He will take me on a supernatural journey continuing what He started July, 2012 in London. I then randomly opened my Bible to the book of Acts, chapter 9, and my eyes went directly to verse 3:

> "As he was nearing Damascus on his mission, a brilliant light from heaven suddenly beamed down on him".

Rich Hopkins

That is what happened to me on July 6, 2012, at "Bank Circle" in London.

So, as we sail the sea of life on God's yacht, we learn to trust God for our provision. We are detached from our past. We are now walking down the "faith" road empowered to conquer our future by using the grace that God has given us.

Jesus said: "according to your faith, so be it" (Matthew 8:13). Say out loud every day the following Biblical declarations to build your faith. They will increase your expectancy of God's goodness, and, thus, increase the manifestation of that goodness in your life.

My prayers are powerful and effective. (2 Cor 5:51; James 5:16)
God richly supplies all my financial needs. (Phil 4:19)
I am dead to sin and alive to obeying God. (Romans 6:11)
I walk in ever-increasing health. (Is 53:3-6)
I live under a supernatural protection. (Ps 91)
I prosper in all my relationships. (Luke 2:52)
I consistently bring God encounters to other people. (Mark 16:17-18T
Through Jesus I am 100% loved and worthy to receive all of God's blessings. (Gal 3:1-5)
Each of my family members is wonderfully blessed & radically loves Jesus. (Acts16:30-1
I uproariously laugh when I hear a lie from the devil. (Ps 2:2-4)

Faith is the evidence of things not seen. (Heb 11:1). Our evidence for things being true is not our circumstances, but God's promises. Say these declarations every day.

I set the course of my life today with my words. (James 3:2-5)
I declare today that I cannot be defeated, discouraged, depressed, or disappointed. (Phil 4:13)

98

I am the head. I have insight. I have wisdom. I have ideas. I have authority. (Deut. 28:13; Deut 8:18; James 1:5-8; Luke 10:19)

As I speak God's promises, they come to pass. They stop all attacks, assaults, oppression, and fear from my life. (2 Peter 1:2-4, Mark 11:23-24)

God is on my side today; therefore I cannot be defeated. (Romans 8:31; Ps 91)

I have the wisdom of God today. I will think the right thoughts, say the right words, and make the right decisions in every situation I face. (1 Cor 2:16)

I choose life today; I choose health. I will not be depressed today. I will not be in lack today. I will not be confused today. (Deut 30:19; Neh 8:10; Ps 103:1-3; 2 Tim 1:6-7)

I expect today to be the best day of my life spiritually, emotionally, relationally, and financially In Jesus' Name. (Romans 15:13)

"God saved you by His special favor when you believed. And you can't take credit for this; it is a gift from God. Salvation is not a reward for the good things we have done, so none of us can boast about it. For we are God's masterpiece. He has created us anew in Christ Jesus, so that we can do the good things he planned for us long ago."

Ephesians 2:8-10
New Living Translation

The Mammon Killer:
A Heart Solution

Now that you have disabled your past and have been empowered to conquer your future by accepting Jesus as your Lord and Savior, let's go a step further in the process of defeating the spirit of mammon. Let's get at it from your heart through the instructions found in the Bible.

Most of us will be facing a major family issue when siblings divide the family inheritance. It will define who is the giver and who is the greedy taker. Addressing two brothers fighting over their inheritance, Jesus said in Luke 12:15 to be on your guard against all kinds of greed; a man's life does not consist in the abundance of possessions.

The Message Bible says in Deuteronomy 15:7-11:

When you happen on someone who is in trouble or needs help among your people with whom you live in this land that God, your God, is giving you, don't look the other way pretending you don't see him. Don't keep a tight grip on your purse. No. Look at him, open your purse, lend whatever and as much as he needs. Don't count the cost. Don't listen to that selfish voice saying, "It's almost the seventh year, the year of All-Debts-Are-Cancelled and turn aside and leave your neighbor in the lurch, refusing to help him. He'll call God's attention to you and your blatant sin. Give freely and spontaneously. Don't have a stingy heart. The way you handle matters like this triggers God, your God's blessing in everything you do, all your work and ventures. There are always going to be poor and needy people among you. So I command you: Always be generous, open purse and hands, give to your neighbors in trouble, your poor and hurting neighbors."

Let's go a step further and look at a conversation between Jesus and a rich young ruler in the Message Bible, Luke 18:18-30.

One day one of the local officials asked him, "Good Teacher, what must I do to deserve eternal life?" Jesus said, "Why are you calling me good? No one is good - only God. You know the commandments, don't you? No illicit sex, no killing, no stealing, no lying, honor your father and mother." He (the rich young Ruler) said, "I've kept them all as long as I can remember." When Jesus heard that he said, "Then there is only one thing left to do. Sell everything you own and give it away to the poor. You will have riches in heaven. Then come, follow me." This was the last thing the official expected to hear. He was very rich and became terribly sad. He was holding on tight to a lot of things and not about to let them go. Seeing his reaction, Jesus said, "Do you have any idea how difficult it is for people who have it all to enter God's kingdom? I'd say it's easier to thread a camel through a needle's eye than get a rich person into God's kingdom."

"Then who has any chance at all?" the others asked.

"No chance at all," Jesus said, "if you think you can pull it off by yourself. Every chance in the world if you trust God to do it."

Peter tried to gain some initiative: "We left everything we owned and followed you, didn't we?"

"Yes," said Jesus, "and you won't regret it. No one who has sacrificed home, spouse, brothers and sisters, parents, children - whatever - will lose out. It will all come back many times over in your lifetime. And then the bonus of eternal life!"

Notice that Jesus said that what you gave away will come back many times over <u>in your lifetime</u> <u>if you trust God</u>. It is likely that it is the spirit of mammon that keeps that from happening in many situations. Jesus does not lie. If He said it, it will happen - <u>if you trust Him</u>. Do not hang on to your possessions. As you get them, give them away. God will see to it that what you give away will be returned. It is an ongoing cycle of giving and receiving. Once in the cycle, there is no thought of fear of lack, no holding on, no hoarding. As you give freely, you receive freely. Just tell the spirit of mammon that puts fear and greed in your spirit to shut up and be gone. This is a spiritual issue. Who will you trust?

<u>To break the hold of the spirit of mammon - GIVE</u>. Step out in faith and give.

Jesus promised that if I ask Him in faith - emphasize faith - for something that is according to His will for me, then it will be provided to me by His grace. Grace means unmerited favor. I don't do anything to earn it or convince God to provide it. He wants to give me whatever I ask for, but He knows what is best for me and He knows my motive for asking. I must ask in childlike faith that He will provide it - not doubting that He hears me and that He wants me to receive it. Through His loving mercy, He responds to my request.

If it is just a matter of asking God to free me from the spirit of mammon, then why was I controlled by it for thirty years as a Christian? Jesus died on the cross to take our sins from us and replace them with the character of God. Why is He allowing me to be controlled by a powerfully destructive spirit? Why ? Because He is a gentleman. He will not remove the spirit of mammon from my life unless I ask Him to do so. Certainly, He doesn't want one of the strongest spirits coming out of hell to be controlling me. God says in His Word to ask Him, truly believing in childlike faith that He will remove it and He will. Yet, I believe that in all those years I never rejected the spirit of mammon. I never truly took authority over it. Instead, I nursed it. I knew it was controlling me. I knew it was separating me from God's will for my life, but I did not speak against it. I did not stand against it and ask God from my heart to free me from it. God knows the condition of my heart and responds accordingly.

How do I stand against it and prove to God that I mean business? The spirit of mammon doesn't want me to know the answer to that question. It wraps me in fear and greed so I can't see the answer. The answer is, however, a principle in the Bible. First, seek God with all my heart and repent for not taking a stand against it. Then, do what the Bible says to do: resist the devil and he will flee. Do it. In this battle, resist the devil by responding in the opposite spirit by giving.

The critical focus of the trading profession is risk/reward, which is the relationship between the amount of risk you take and the return you expect to receive for taking that risk. It is measured in dollars and cents, in price. You don't take the risk unless there is a definable and acceptable probability of adequate return. The principle focus of giving requires a much different, almost opposite, motivation and expectation. Do not give with the expectation of receiving; give with the expectation of blessing others with no strings attached. I am not giving to get; I are giving to bless. My return is in my heart - the joy of helping someone.

Allowing my giving to break the spirit of mammon requires faith, persistent faith. I must let go of what I am fearful of losing and give away what I worked so hard to get. To my mind, that was a contradiction. The spirit of mammon tells my fearful mind that I can't pay my bills if I give it (time, money, possessions) away or it tells my greedy mind that what I want or have is a reward for my hard work, so why should I deny myself the luxury of it. All I am thinking about is me. Instead, I must think from my heart where the spirit of God speaks to me. I listen for what God wants me to do with the "money". <u>It changes from mammon to money as I see it from God's perspective.</u> The power of mammon is broken as I give God's way in faith. The fears and greedy attitudes that I have experienced under the spirit of mammon's influence are unfounded. God promises a blessing to those who give. Have the faith to believe it and it will happen.

There is a change of personality that comes with casting the spirit of mammon out of my soul - my mind, will, and emotions. I have been absorbed by a focus on myself as I try to overcome the spirit of mammon. Fear & greed jaded my perspective on life, leaving me down and out, helpless. When I step out of my shadow - out of darkness - and come into God's light and give to someone, I literally come alive. I give with financial help, with my words of encouragement, with my listening attention and ideas, with any type of helpful communication. I build a two-way relationship and become the giver in the relationship instead of the taker that I am accustomed to being. I made it a new habit to develop at least one new relationship a month, making sure it is a growing relationship, not here today and gone tomorrow. As my network of relationships that requires giving of myself grows, I will not focus on myself and the spirit of mammon. Thinking about money changes to how can I bless my relationships. No longer am I obsessed with mammon's taunting "will I have enough?" or "how can I get more?"

I encourage you to read another perspective on the spirit of mammon than my own. Sam Polk, a thirty-year old Wall Street bond trader, wrote his story for the New York Times on January 19, 2014. He reveals the greed side of the spirit of mammon, which is a more typical Wall Street story than my "buy side" story originating from fear. Ironically, during a portion of his career he traded corporate bonds, which, if he had traded in the early 1980's (which he didn't), he could have been the other side of my State of Cal PERS corporate bond purchases. Because he is not sharing a Christian perspective, he doesn't refer to the addiction he lived in as the spirit of mammon. However, his focus on money was also more than just a means of exchange. He was driven to get more and more money, far more than he needed. Fortunately, he saw the destructive power it had over him and walked away from it.

Sam wrote that he made millions of dollars as a single man in his late 20's with no children or financial obligations. He compared it to an alcoholic needing another drink. It was an addiction. He said he worked like a maniac as a bond trader - like I did. His girlfriend said "adios", as did mine for the same reason. His counselor told him to stop focusing on money and heal the wounds of his personal life that caused his need for power that trading satisfied. Was it his from his childhood? Did he have an absent dad? I don't know, but he responded to his counselor by going for more money and became what he called "a fireball of greed".

Eventually, Sam found redemption. Through the healing of his inner wounds and his previous awareness of the characteristics of addiction, he walked away from Wall Street. He is now happily married raising a family. He started a nonprofit called "Groceryships" (groceryships. com) to help poor families overcome food addiction. His focus, his heart is GIVING.

"What I'm trying to do here is to get you to relax, to not be so preoccupied with getting, so you can respond to God's giving. People who don't know God and the way he works fuss over these things, but you know both God and how he works. Steep your life in God reality, God-initiatives, God -provisions. Don't worry about missing out. You'll find that all your everyday human concerns will be met. Give your entire attention to what God is doing right now, and don't get worked up about what may or may not happen tomorrow. God will help you deal with whatever hard things come up when the time comes."

Matthew 6:31-34
The Message Bible in Contemporary English

Finding Peace and Contentment:
The Mind of Heaven

By now you have an understanding of who I am. I have put before you the events of my life and how I responded to them. The result was a search for peace and contentment. Do you see yourself somewhere in the book? I hope so because I have written this intimate look at my history for you. We should all live in peace and contentment, but few do. I spent nearly a lifetime trying to find it without success.

God was trying to lead me into peace and contentment when He told me in 1988 that He was moving us to Phoenix to teach me mercy and meekness. (page 50 above) In teaching me mercy, He wanted to teach me compassion for others. The material realm had consumed me. I was measuring my self-worth by our competitive American society's standards that says you are what you have or don't have. He was able to teach me mercy - to live in His mercy, not just know about it - when I lived for three months at a YWAM base in Kona, Hawaii (page 61-62 above). Unfortunately, that was an experience, not a lifestyle. Three years later, He sent me to a church in Phoenix to put me in circumstances where I had to express mercy. Then, as if to emphasize its importance, I received a double portion in June 2012 when we traveled across Europe as YWAM'ers. Unfortunately, June 2012 was twenty-four years after we moved to Phoenix. During those years I was in survivor mode living under the spirit of mammon. Despite the many church ministries, I was unwilling to hunger and thirst for God enough to give up "me" and trust Him completely to be rid of mammon's control. I finally sought Him with all my heart - and, through His forgiving mercy, He received me. Giving that same mercy, that compassion, to others is a source of peace and contentment. The merciful receive mercy. I finally found peace and contentment.

Finding meekness, however, required a personality change. I was a demanding, self-centered, fearful bond trader. I was a lonely mess. I lacked the flexibility of relationship skills. I needed meekness. Meekness means you are willing to submit to the ideas of others for the good of the group. It is not a sign of weakness. It is displayed by not always having to have it your way. That was hard for me as a bond trader because I was always the contrarian. I lived by the adage "if its in print, it is too late", meaning that it's already "priced in the market". I was trained to see the other side of the coin, which is usually negative. I found it hard to agree with the group. I became somewhat combative, certainly contrarian. I was argumentative. I assumed people spoke with "forked tongue" because of my experience with Wall Street at Cal PERS. The spirit of mammon was driving me in greed and fear to "beat" the market - an obsession - at whatever the cost. Over time my dominant personality lost all display of meekness. The good news is that I finally found it and I want you to find it too. How? Be submissive. You don't have to loose your position in your group; just learn to listen and relinquish control.

Our trip to Europe in 2012 was a supernatural exercise in learning to "listen" - to not be controlled by "me". The spirit of mammon had controlled me throughout my financial futures trading for over thirty years, blinded by a distorted, prideful view of my ability. I am still using the same basic trading system to beat the market that I used at Cal PERS. That system was my identity. I am ashamed to admit that it had an even higher importance than my relationship with God. I could not hear what God wanted me to do. My trading system told me what to do. I was locked into the pride of MY system. The supernatural experience at "Bank Circle" in London was a confirmation from God that I had begun the process of finding meekness and being the person God wants me to be, living in peace and contentment, and walking in the purpose God intended for me.

I recently heard the Holy Spirit tell me to read Isaiah 23. I remembered that He told me to read that chapter on a mountaintop New Years' Day prayer time in 1989, not long after we moved to Phoenix. It hit me strongly back then because it talks of the judgment and destruction of Tyre by God because of their pride. Tyre was known for its trading. The end of the chapter says Tyre will be back again in seventy years trading as before, but the profits will go to God and His Kingdom. Isaiah 23 was very much on my heart for a few years, but has long since been forgotten. I did not hear what God was telling me. My ego was in control. It was not coincidental that there were no profits to speak of in my trading all those twenty-four years. It was a useless effort. Could my "seventy years" be ending? So far, the answer is "yes" based on my trading since the Bank Circle Encounter. I have learned to listen to God instead of my trading system. Meekness has overcome pride. With meekness comes peace and contentment.

Now that I have learned a very simplistic way to find peace and contentment, let's learn how to take authority over the spirit of mammon so that it does not return. Let's go back to my childhood. My Mom used to describe me as the fastest race horse at the starting gate. I was so anxious to win the race that I accidentally kicked the front portion of the gate that opens at the beginning of the race. I bruised my leg; I didn't win the race. She was trying to tell me to look before I leap and not be impulsive. I heard it differently. As a child I took it too mean I would fail. A voice inside me said I was not good enough. I agreed. As an adult, the lie continues as fear and shame. Thinking I was not "good enough" created fear that I would fail, which translated into loosing money in trading. Trading requires quick, confident, disciplined decision-making - the antithesis of fear-based trading. That fear emotion deep in my soul was re-enforced by my failed marriage over forty years ago that was caused by my prideful ego desiring control (see page 38). I was enveloped in shame. The hurts of my past resulted in a behavior that became my identity. The spirit of mammon reinforced that failure mentality. For over thirty-five years I labeled myself a failure when I had a loosing trade. Unfortunately, in the real "trader" world, you have to loose money on some trades - just win big on winners and loose small on losers. The spirit of mammon torment made that hard to do. I expected perfectionism that doesn't exist. I was driven to perform when the odds said I would fail and, as a result, I became that person - a failure. I was in a cycle of failure that became my identity. To get out of that cycle, I had to see and speak and believe who God made me to be.

When Jesus Christ fills your heart with His love, you see through the lies and destroy them. The Bible says that His perfect love casts out fear. As my life story reveals, letting the perfect love of Jesus fill my heart is not a simple task. In fact, it is not a task. It is an evolving change in my identity as I come to believe in my mind and spirit that I am, in fact, who God made me to be, not who the spirit of mammon makes me believe I am. You may or may not remember negative words spoken to you in your childhood, but they are probably there and are the root cause of your negative self-image. At the end of this chapter is a partial list of verses from the Bible that describes who God made you to be. That is who you are, not how the spirit of mammon defines you. <u>Speak out loud through the list every day.</u> Be disciplined. <u>As you speak it, you will believe it, and as you believe it, you will become it.</u> It took me much longer than it should have to complete that process because my identity was so bound into the spirit of mammon. The "racehorse" in me was still trying to win the race, but I had a lame leg. The racehorse in me was the need to be recognized, to be significant. I needed to win the race, but how could I with a lame leg. I had to change the vision I had of myself. So I drew a detailed mental picture of myself winning the race and began speaking about how I'm going to win it. I am who God says I am. If I am who God made me to be, <u>I WILL WIN THE RACE</u>.

The spirit of mammon had control over my purpose and destiny by controlling who I thought I was and what I thought I needed to have and do. It controlled my spirit by being dominant. My relationship with the spirit of mammon was stronger than my relationship with God. Deep inside, I believed what the spirit of mammon was telling me more than I believed what the Bible says. I believed mammon's lies for over thirty years.

Overcome the passivity that is the result of a beaten-down life. Pull yourself up and stand against mammon's lie. Just do it!

If you are under pressure to "perform" that seems insurmountable, release the pressure to God and it will be manageable as you develop perseverance. God uses the process of persevering the situation to develop a depth of proven character that produces hope. Hope doesn't disappoint. It takes you out of survivor mode and opens the door for favor. Start saying things that are hope-filled and you will overcome your obstacles. To attain your goals and to fulfill your dreams, your future needs the right vocabulary coming out of your mouth. Speak faith. Believe that you are overcoming the obstacle. The favor of God will reign in your life as you ask Him to provide your need and faithfully trust Him to do so. The Bible says that faith is the substance of things hoped for, the evidence of things not seen. Hope is an influential power. Expect good things to happen. Expectation is the atmosphere of the miraculous. If you are expecting, you won't be disappointed. Hope comes from God, not the circumstances. Hope comes when you feed God's promises to your soul. You are made to be full of hope, for the Bible says that without hope the heart grows sick. Don't beg God for it; instead, radically declare it. Demand it to happen!!

Speaking God's promises out loud speaks hope. As you speak, you feed your soul - your mind, will, and emotions - a vocabulary of positive victorious words. Speak them repeatedly until they are part of you. For example, you are fifty-five and fearful that you are too old for the job. No, scratch that thought! Say repeatedly that I am young and able. I have experience and maturity that others don't have. I am valuable and ready to meet any challenge and conquer it. Say it, say it, say it. What you speak you are and get!

The events of my life caused me to be an unsuccessful trader. It took a long time, longer than it should have, but the door finally closed on a failed career. I traded my life away - thirty-five years of it. BUT...a new door has opened for the life of a giving optimist...healed of my past. All things worked together for my ultimate good. I don't worry about where I am or fret about where I have or haven't been. Instead, I look into the eyes of those around me and wonder where THEY are and how I can be a blessing to them. That's all that counts.

My life story is certainly not over. I have narrated a life that started full of hope and confidence. A devastating, self-inflicted divorce stole my optimism and introduced me to a demonic spirit - the spirit of mammon. The consuming lust for money through trading bonds created a mask to hide the hurt of divorce. The drive for mammon became an addiction that controlled me for thirty-five years, thirty of those years as a Christian.

How could a faithful Christian be controlled by a demonic spirit? Outwardly, I was comfortable in my state of torment. To be rid of it, all I had to do was stand up to it and command it to leave. As a Christian I have that authority and power, but I was blinded by money's enticements. More important, however, I did not have a close Father-son relationship with my Heavenly Father because of my distant relationship with my earthly father. I did not have the trust to rely on my Heavenly Father to intervene and help me break the hold the spirit of mammon had on me.

The good news is that the spirit of mammon has finally lost its hold. During our month in France and Germany, I enjoyed an atmosphere of freedom. I was free from the bond market. Our life at home did not exist. I was free from a spirit of lack because our trip was basically paid for in advance. I was in a Christian environment where the focus was ministering to other people. I saw the hurts of others instead of living in mine. Once the focus was off me, God could do His work, recreating the Rich Hopkins that He created before I was born. As the spirit of mammon comes off of me, my Godly purpose comes forth.

God allows us to go through trials to develop our character and to help others go through similar trials. As I walk into a mammon-free life, I am called with a listening ear and an empathetic heart to help those controlled by the spirit of mammon. Further, I am called to a much more pervasive need - the fatherless, as I described in the Family chapter. Not having a close relationship with an earthly father has created an epidemic of hurting men, which will be the subject of my next book.

For now, I am called to comfort with "international compassion" those reading these pages. Please email me at rich@tradingyourlifeaway.com.

King Solomon, in his biblical book of Ecclesiastes, summarized his quest for inner peace by concluding that it can only be found in God. He says that whatever you chase will end in disappointment if it is the sole reason for your existence. My chase was money, and I traded my life away trying to get it.

My original intent in writing this little book was to explain to my kids and grandkids what I learned from a failed career. Well, to be objective, I myopically allowed the impersonal "market" to determine my destiny. The needs and personalities of people were not relevant. I was the "need". As I said at the beginning of this narrative, living at the beginning of the "baby-boom" generation was a wonderful opportunity to see the needs of my generation and fill them. Instead, I was controlled by the love of money - the spirit of mammon.

King Solomon, the wisest man on earth in his day, concluded that peace and contentment can only be found by fearing (respecting) God and obeying His commands. I was trying to serve two masters, God and money. Jesus said that that was not possible. When I was serving God, I was truly in peace and contentment - the peace that passes all understanding. I remember ministering to the homeless and downtrodden under the San Francisco freeways. Likewise Vietnamese refugees in Phoenix. Or ministering on the prayer team to the hurts of people in church. But that was weekends. What about when the market was trading?

NOW FREE FROM THE SPIRIT OF MAMMON:

When I start looking at the trading screen, I take my thoughts captive. No fear, no greed.

I listen to the conviction in my heart where the Holy Spirit resides.

I relate to those around me in all meekness and mercy.

I give my love. I give my time and attention. I give my life's experiences.

I give materially.

WHO ARE YOU NOW?

Below are descriptions of who you became when you said the prayer on pages 90-91. Speak these Biblical promises out loud every day. As you do, you will peel off who the spirit of mammon says you are and replace it with who God says you are. Be disciplined. As you speak it, you will believe it, and as you believe it, you will become it.

I am greatly loved by God. Romans 1:7; Ephesians 2:4; Colossians 3:12; 1 Thessalonians 1:4

I am God's child. John 1:12

I am God's friend. John 15:15

I am God's workmanship. Ephesians 2:10

I am God's coworker. 1 Corinthians 3:9

I am God's select, full of mercy, kindness, humility, and longsuffering. Romans 8:33

I am holy and without blame before Him in love. Ephesians 1:4

I am forgiven of all my sins. Colossians 3:12

I am alive with Christ. Ephesians 2:5

I am united with God and am one spirit with Him. 1 Corinthians 6:17

I am seated with Christ in the heavenly realm. Ephesians 2:6

I am assured that all things work together for my good. Romans 8:28

I am free from condemnation. Romans 8:1,2

I have direct access to God through the Holy Spirit. Ephesians 2:1

I can apporach God with freedom and confidence Ephesians 3:12

I can do all things through Christ who strengthens me. Philippeans 4:13

I cannot be separated from the love of God. Romans 8:35

I have not been given a spirit of fear, but rather of power, love, and a sound mind 2 Timothy 2:17

I have the mind of Christ. 1 Corinthians 2:16; Philippeans 2:5

I am far from oppression and fear does not come near me. Isaiah 54:14

I have the peace of God that passes all understanding. Philippeans 4:7

I have no lack for my God supplies all my need. Philippeans 4:19

I am submitted to God; therefore the devil flees from me because I resist him in the name of Jesus. James 4:7

I am born of God; therefore satan does not touch me. 1 John 5:18

I am redeemed from the curse of sin, sickness, and poverty. Deuteronomy 28:15-68; Galatians 3:13

Some Verses To Live By From The Bible, God's Word To Us

<u>(reread my story and see how I did or did not live by them)</u>

ISAIAH 48:17 (MSG): I am God, your God, who teaches you how to live right and well. I show you what to do, where to go.

PSALM 35:27 The Lord delights in the prosperity of His servants (you & I).

PROVERBS 16:7 (NLT): When the ways of people please the Lord, He makes even their enemies be at peace with them. (I am only now "releasing" the paranoia of the person trading against me, and, as a result, I will see his influence leave.)

PROVERBS 3:6-7 (MSG): Trust God from the bottom of your heart; don't try to figure out everything on your own. Listen for God's voice in everything you do, everywhere you go; He's the one who will keep you on track. Don't assume that you know it all. (My life's verse. (Throughout the last 31 years, when I let go and let God, I stayed on track.)

JAMES 1:5-8 (NLT): If you need wisdom - if you want to know what God wants you to do - ask Him, and He will gladly tell you.

He will not resent you asking. But when you ask Him, be sure you really expect Him to answer, for a doubtful mind is as unsettled as a wave of the sea that is driven and tossed by the wind. People like that should not expect to receive anything from the Lord. They can't make up their minds. They waver back and forth in everything they do. (Going to YWAM-Kona was a perfect example. I never questioned it. But there have been many blessings missed because He told me to do something and I didn't act because of fear. I wasn't sure whether I heard Him or heard my own desires, so I did nothing - I doubted.)

JEREMIAH 29:12-13 (MSG): When you call on Me, when you come and pray to Me, I'll listen. When you come looking for Me, you'll find Me. Yes, when you get serious about finding Me and want it more than anything else, I'll make sure you won't be disappointed. God's Decree. I'll turn things around for you. (When I received Jesus as my Lord & Savior in 1982 and when I got the job in San Francisco after giving up our Denver home are two examples of many.)

DEUTERONOMY 8:17-18 (MSG): If you start thinking to yourselves, "I did all this. And all by myself. I'm rich. It's all mine!" - well, think again. Remember that God, your God, gave you the strength to produce all this wealth so as to confirm the covenant that He promised to your ancestors - as it is today. If you forget God, your God, and start taking up with other gods (example: money, yourself), serving and worshiping them, I'm on the record right now as giving you firm warning: that will be the end of you; I mean it - destruction. (I did not seek the Lord when I decided to take the job in Albuquerque! I took it for money!)

LUKE 12:33-34 (MSG): Be generous. Give to the poor. Get yourselves a bank that can't go bankrupt, a bank in heaven far from bank robbers, safe from embezzlers, a bank you can bank on. It's obvious, isn't it? The place where your treasure is is the place where you will most want to be, and end up being. (Being mammonized?)

MATTHEW 6:19-21 (MSG): Don't hoard treasure down here where it gets eaten by moths and corroded by rust - or worse! - stolen by burglars. Stockpile treasure in heaven where it is safe from moths and rust and burglars. It's obvious isn't it? The place where your treasure is, is the place where you most want to be, and end up being. (Being mammonized!)

MATTHEW 6:24-26 (MSG): You can't worship two gods at once. Loving one God you will end up hating the other. Adoration for one feeds contempt for the other. You can't worship God and Money (mammon) both. (Being mammonized!)

MATTHEW 6:30-34 (MSG): If God gives such attention to the appearance of wildflowers - most of which are never even seen - don't you think He will attend to you, take pride in you, do His best for you? What I am trying to do here is to get you to relax, to not be so preoccupied with getting, so you can respond to God's giving. People who don't know God and the way He works fuss over these things, but you know both God and how He works. Steep your life in God-reality, God-initiative, God-provisions. Don't worry about missing out. You'll find all your everyday human concerns will be met. Give your entire attention to what God is doing right now, and don't get worked up about what may or may not happen tomorrow. God will help you deal with whatever hard things come up when the time comes. (Didn't happen when I was being mammonized!)

PSALM 25:12 (MSG): When you keep your eyes on God, you won't trip over your own feet.

MATTHEW 11:28-30 (MSG): Jesus said: Are you tired? Burned out? Come to me. Get away with Me and you'll recover your life.

I'll show you how to take a real rest. Walk with Me and work with Me - watch how I do it. Learn the unforced rhythms of grace. I won't lay anything heavy or ill-fitting on you. Keep company with Me and you'll learn to live freely & lightly. (My Christian life when I, in fact, would walk with Him.)

COLOSSIANS 1:13 (NLT): God has rescued us from the one who rules in the kingdom of darkness (satan), and He has brought us into the Kingdom of His dear Son (Jesus). Jesus has purchased us with His Blood (on the cross at Calvary) and has forgiven all our sins.

PHILIPPIANS 4:6-8 (NLT): Don't worry about anything; instead, pray about everything. Tell God what you need, and thank Him for all He has done. If you do this, you will experience God's peace, which is far more wonderful than the human mind can understand. His peace will guard your heart and mind as you live in Christ Jesus. (I did not do this concerning the incident in San Francisco that caused me to leave the job God gave me.)

1 PETER 5:5-7 (NLT): You younger men, accept the authority of the elders. And all of you, serve each other in humility, for God sets Himself against the proud, but He shows favor to the humble. So humble yourselves under the mighty power of God, and in His good time He will honor you. Give all your worries and cares to God, for He cares about what happens to you. (The lack of humility caused by fear and worry has hurt me in jobs and trading. Humility requires confidence in who you are.)

PROVERBS 11:25 (MSG): The generous prosper and are satisfied; those who refresh others will themselves be refreshed. (Can't do it when you are mammonized)

LUKE 6:38 (MSG): Give away your life; you will find life given back, but not merely given back - given back with bonus and blessing.

Giving, not getting, is the way. Generosity begets generosity. (The lack of giving has been a personality weakness since I began trading -fear of loss -spirit of mammon.)

2 CORINTHIANS 9:6-8 (NLT): Remember this - a farmer who plants only a few seed will get a small crop. But the one who plants generously will get a generous crop. You must each make up your mind as to how much you should give. Don't give reluctantly or in response to pressure. For God loves the person who gives cheerfully. And God will provide cheerfully all you need. Then you will always have everything you need and plenty left over to share with others.

2 PETER 1:3-9 (NLT): As we know Jesus better, His divine power gives us everything we need for living a godly life. He has called us to receive His own glory and goodness! And by that same mighty power, He has given us all of His rich & wonderful promises. He has promised that you will escape the decadence all around you caused by evil desires and that you will share in His divine nature. So make every effort to apply the benefits of these promises to your life. Then your faith will produce a life of moral excellence. A life of moral excellence leads to knowing God better. Knowing God leads to self-control. Self-control leads to endurance, and patient endurance leads to godliness. Godliness leads to love for others, and finally you will grow to have genuine love for everyone. The more you grow like this, the more you will become productive and useful in your knowledge of our Lord Jesus Christ. But those who fail to develop these virtues are blind or, at least, very shortsighted. They have already forgotten that God has cleansed them from their old life of sin.

JAMES 5:19-20 (MSG): My dear friends, if you know people who have wandered off from God's truth, don't write them off. Go after them. Get them back and you will have rescued precious lives from destruction and prevented an epidemic of wandering away from God.

MATTHEW 6:1-2 (NLT): Take care! Don't do your good deeds publicly, to be admired, because then you will loose the reward from your Father in heaven. When you give a gift to someone in need, don't shout about it as the hypocrites do - blowing trumpets in the synagogues and streets to call attention to their acts of charity! I assure you, they have received all the reward they will ever get.

Bibliography

Duncan, Suzanne Lynn, "The Love of Money: Why Greed Isn't Always Good", State Street Center for Applied Research, 'love of money research', 2016

Gamblers Anonymous International, 20 questions, gamblers anonymous.org,

Hauck, D.W., "Alchemy of the Paranormal", www.alchemylab.com

Hill, Craig and Pitts, Earl, Wealth Riches and,, Money, Littleton, CO, Family Foundations Int, 2003

Leaf, Caroline, Switch on Your Brain: The Key to Peak Happiness, Thinking, & Health, Baker   Books, Grand Rapids, MI 49516 2013

LeVang, Curtis, Looking Good Outside- Feeling Bad Inside, YWAM Publishing, 1995 out-of-print

McCray, Allen, Whose Behind the Mask? Becoming Who You Have Always Been But Were Never Allowed To Be, Bloomington, IN 47403 2014

Morris, Robert, <u>The Blessed Life: Unlocking the Rewards of Generous Living,</u> Baker Publishing Group, Grand Rapids, MI 49516 2004

Robinson, Bryan E., <u>Work Addiction-Hidden Legacies of Adult Children,</u> Health Communications, Deerfield Beach,FL 1989

Zadai, Kevin, <u>A Meeting Place With God: The Heavenly Encounter Series, Vol 1,</u> Warrior Notes, 2017.

Printed in the United States
By Bookmasters